STAAR

STATE OF TEXAS ASSESSMENTS OF ACADEMIC READINESS

GRADE 5
READING SKILLS

First Edition

Table of Contents

Introduction

About the English Language Arts Literacy STAAR Tests

The English Language Arts Literacy Grade 5 test includes a total of 50 questions. The reading test consists of texts and poems, with questions directly related to these written passages. To respond accurately, students must carefully read and comprehend the material. They have the option to revisit the texts for reference when checking for specific details.

About the English Language Arts Literacy Tests in This Book

The 5 practice tests included in this book are designed to replicate the ELA STAAR tests accurately. They provide your child with a valuable opportunity to understand key concepts and familiarize themselves with the format, types of questions, and time constraints they will encounter on the STAAR test. Repetition is a proven method for effective studying. We firmly believe in the power of practice, which is why we've included five carefully crafted practice tests in this book.

By working through these practice tests, your child can:

- **Improve time management:** They will become adept at managing their time efficiently during the test, ensuring they complete all sections within the allocated time.
- **Build confidence:** Repeatedly solving questions in a format similar to the actual test will boost their confidence, reducing anxiety on test day.

- **Identify weaknesses:** These tests will help pinpoint specific areas where your child may need additional review and practice.
- **Enhance problem-solving skills:** Regular practice hones problem-solving skills and strategies, enabling your child to tackle challenging questions effectively.
- **Score higher:** Through focused practice and familiarization with the test structure, your child can strive for higher scores on the STAAR test.

The questions in these practice tests closely mirror those found in the actual STAAR tests, ensuring that your child gains a deep understanding of the test's structure and content. By working through these practice tests, they will be well-equipped to achieve success on the ELA STAAR test.

As parents, educators, or instructors, your support and encouragement play a pivotal role in your child's academic journey. We encourage you to actively engage with your child's ELA education, using these resources as tools to enhance their learning experience.

Dear Parents,

Thank you for purchasing the STAAR Reading Practice Workbook for Grade 5.

As an independent author, I have put a great deal of effort into ensuring the quality and accuracy of the content provided. Each problem has been carefully solved and reviewed to provide the best learning experience.

However, despite the rigorous efforts to maintain high standards, occasional mistakes can occur. If you come across any errors or discrepancies in the book or the solutions, please do not hesitate to reach out. Your feedback is invaluable in helping to improve the quality of this workbook.

For any corrections, questions, or comments, please contact me at *jasonreedbooks@gmail.com*. Your assistance in identifying and rectifying any issues is greatly appreciated.

Thank you for your understanding and support.

Sincerely,

Jason Reed

PRACTICE TEST 1

GET STARTED →

Read the following passage and answer the questions below.

(1) Once upon a time, in a small log cabin in a place called Kentucky, there lived a boy named Abraham Lincoln. He was born on February 12, 1809, in a humble family. Abe, as everyone called him, had a thirst for knowledge and loved to read books. But his life was not easy; his family was poor, and they had to work hard just to make a living.

(2) Abe's determination and love for learning led him to become a self-taught scholar. He studied law and became a lawyer, always believing in fairness and justice. But what made him truly famous was his role as the 16th President of the United States.

(3) In 1860, Abraham Lincoln was elected as president, and he faced a big challenge – the country was divided over important issues, especially slavery. Abe believed that all people should be treated equally, no matter the color of their skin. He worked tirelessly to unite the nation, and even during the Civil War, he never gave up on his dream of ending slavery.

(4) One of the most famous things about Abraham Lincoln is the Emancipation Proclamation. This important document declared that all enslaved people in the Confederate states were free. It was a huge step towards ending slavery in the United States.

(5) Abraham Lincoln was also known for his famous Gettysburg Address, a short speech he gave at a battlefield in Pennsylvania. In it, he talked about the importance of freedom and equality, saying, "government of the people, by the people, for the people, shall not perish from the earth." These words are still remembered and cherished today.

(6) Sadly, Abraham Lincoln's life was cut short when he was assassinated in 1865, just days after the Civil War ended. But his legacy lives on. He is remembered as one of (7) America's greatest presidents, a symbol of honesty, determination, and the belief that anyone can make a difference, no matter where they come from. So, the next time you see a picture of Abraham Lincoln or a five-dollar bill with his face on it, remember the amazing story of this real-life hero who changed the world with his kindness and his belief in freedom and equality for all.

1. What is the most likely reason the author wrote this story?

(A) To compare Abraham Lincoln to other American Presidents.

(B) To inform the reader about the troubles of slavery.

(C) To explain the meaning behind the Gettysburg Address.

(D) To teach the reader about the life of Abraham Lincoln

2. What is one reason the author presents the information in the article in chronological order? Support your answer with evidence from the article.

_____

_____

_____

_____

_____

_____

_____

_____

_____

_____

_____

3. What is most closely a synonym for "humble" as used in paragraph 1?

(A) Wealthy

(B) Modest

(C) Extravagant

(D) Political

4. What is the key idea of paragraph 4?

(A) The Emancipation Proclamation was incredibly important in the fight against slavery.

(B) Lincoln was a well-loved President of the U.S.A.

(C) Sadly, Lincoln was assassinated in 1865.

(D) We can remember the legacy of Lincoln every time we look at the $5 bill.

5. Based on information in paragraph 6 and paragraph 7, the reader can conclude that–

(A) Lincoln helped to end slavery with the Emancipation Proclamation.

(B) Abraham grew up in a very poor family.

(C) The bravery and courage Lincoln showed in his life live on even today.

(D) Abraham Lincoln is known for his long beard and tall hat.

6. Which sentence is used to support the idea that Lincoln believed slavery was wrong?

A. Abe's determination and love for learning led him to become a self-taught scholar.

B. Abe believed that all people should be treated equally, no matter the color of their skin.

C. America's greatest presidents, a symbol of honesty, determination, and the belief that anyone can make a difference, no matter where they come from.

D. But his life was not easy; his family was poor, and they had to work hard just to make a living.

7. How is information organized in paragraph 7?

A. It is the chronological depiction of Lincoln's run for President.

B. It compares and contrasts Lincoln's upbringing with his adulthood.

C. It summarizes the article and explains what the key points are to remember.

D. Cause and effect of the Emancipation Proclamation.

Read the next two selections. Then choose the best answer to each question.

Off To Camp

(1) One sunny summer morning, in the heart of the woods, there was a fifth-grader named Emma who was off to the most exciting adventure of her life – summer camp. With her backpack slung over her shoulder and a heart full of anticipation, she arrived at Camp Pineview, nestled near a sparkling lake.

(2) Camp Pineview was a magical place, surrounded by towering pine trees and filled with the laughter of kids from all over the place. Emma's cabin was cozy and smelled of fresh pine, with bunk beds, a warm fireplace, and a big window that looked out into the forest.

(3) On the first day of camp, Emma was assigned to the Bluebird cabin. She met her cabin mates, Sarah, Lily, and Jake, and they quickly became fast friends. Together, they went on unforgettable adventures, from hiking through the dense forest to roasting marshmallows by the campfire.

(4) One day, the camp counselors announced a scavenger hunt. The teams were chosen, and Emma found herself on the "Wild Explorers" team with her new friends. They were given a list of items to find in the woods, like a pinecone, a feather, and a special blue wildflower.

(5) As they ventured deeper into the forest, Emma's heart raced with excitement. They found the pinecone near a babbling brook, and Lily spotted a feather stuck to a bush. But the blue wildflower proved elusive. They searched high and low, through bushes and under rocks, but it seemed as if it had vanished.

(6) Just when they were about to give up, Emma remembered something. She had read about a special blue wildflower in a book she brought from home. She described it to her team, and they realized they had been searching for the wrong flower all along. With newfound determination, they followed Emma's directions and found the elusive blue wildflower.

(7) Their team won the scavenger hunt, and they celebrated their victory with s'mores and campfire stories that night. Emma felt proud and grateful for her new friends and the unforgettable adventures at Camp Pineview.

(8) As the days turned into weeks, Emma learned valuable lessons about teamwork, courage, and the beauty of nature. She discovered that the best part of camp was not just the exciting activities but the friendships she had made along the way. And so, with a heart full of cherished memories, Emma knew that Camp Pineview would always hold a special place in her heart, and she couldn't wait to return next summer for more adventures and new friendships.

Calibrating Computers

(1) Computers are like our modern-day wizards, performing incredible feats of technology and helping us in countless ways. These magical machines come in various shapes and sizes, from tiny smartphones to powerful desktop computers. They have become an essential part of our lives, helping us learn, work, and play.

(2) One of the most fascinating things about computers is their ability to process information at incredible speeds. They can solve complex problems, perform mathematical calculations, and even play games with us. This super-fast thinking is thanks to the tiny electronic brains inside them called microchips.

(3) Computers also help us communicate with people all over the world. Whether it's sending an email to a friend, chatting with someone in a different country, or joining a video call with family, computers have brought us closer together. They can even translate languages for us, making it easier to connect with people from different cultures.

(4) Another exciting aspect of computers is their creativity. They can help us make art, compose music, and design amazing buildings. They allow us to create and explore imaginary worlds in video games or simulate real-life scenarios for learning and training.

(5) In our everyday lives, computers make tasks more manageable. They help doctors diagnose illnesses, allow us to shop online, and even help control the temperature in our homes. They have truly transformed the way we live, work, and play, making them one of the most incredible inventions of our time. So, whether you're doing homework, playing games, or just exploring the vast world of information on the internet, remember that computers are like your reliable partners in the digital age, ready to assist you with their magical abilities.

8. The phrase "heart full of anticipation" used in paragraph 1 in "Off To Camp" tells us what about Emma?

(A) She is dreading going to camp.

(B) Camp last year was really fun.

(C) She is very excited to go to camp.

(D) Camp will be filled with lots of bugs and insects.

9. What was Emma's main lesson in "Off To Camp"?

(A) Camp activities are always fun and physical.

(B) It's important to know about the different flowers that grow in the forest.

(C) Sometimes summer camp can be difficult, but you should go again each year to see if it gets better.

(D) Teamwork and friendship are important in life.

10. Read paragraph 7 again from "Off To Camp". Which sentence below would NOT fit well into this paragraph?

(7) Their team won the scavenger hunt, and they celebrated their victory with s'mores and campfire stories that night. Emma felt proud and grateful for her new friends and the unforgettable adventures at Camp Pineview.

(A) She would always remember the fun they had finding all of the scavenger items.

(B) Emma's mom and dad were worried about Emma being away at camp.

(C) Emma and her friends stayed up all night telling scary stories.

(D) The s'mores were delicious, but messy!

11. How is paragraph 4 important to the plot of the story "Off To Camp"?

(A) It sets up one of the adventures Emma and her new friends will have at camp.

(B) It explains how the camp from previous years had been for Emma.

(C) It's when Emma realizes that her new friends are not very kind.

(D) It shows how excited Emma is to go to summer camp this year.

12. What does paragraph 8 in "Off To Camp" tell us about what will happen next?

(A) Emma will go home to her parents.

(B) This is the last summer camp event for Emma.

(C) Summer camp will happen again next year.

(D) Emma and her friends will keep in touch all year long.

13. What are TWO things computers can do better than humans, according to "Calibrating Computers"?

(A) Process information quicker.

(B) Solve complex mathematical problems easily.

(C) Help to make vegetables grow better in your garden.

(D) Teach you how to drive a car.

14. What is the central idea of the article "Calibrating Computers"?

(A) Computers can be incredibly expensive to buy.

(B) The first computer was huge and took up an entire room.

(C) Computers can help make our daily lives easier.

(D) Computer coding is a good career to go into.

15. Read paragraph 3 again from "Calibrating Computers". What is an assumption being made for the author to include this paragraph?

(3) Computers also help us communicate with people all over the world. Whether it's sending an email to a friend, chatting with someone in a different country, or joining a video call with family, computers have brought us closer together. They can even translate languages for us, making it easier to connect with people from different cultures.

(A) Foreign languages can be easy to learn.

(B) Having friends in other countries is really important in our lives.

(C) Sending mail takes too long if you're sending it to other countries.

(D) It can be difficult to communicate with your friends in other countries.

16. Which sentence helps us understand how computers work in the article "Calibrating Computers"?

(A) They can solve complex problems, perform mathematical calculations, and even play games with us.

(B) This super-fast thinking is thanks to the tiny electronic brains inside them called microchips.

(C) Computers also help us communicate with people all over the world.

(D) Whether it's sending an email to a friend, chatting with someone in a different country, or joining a video call with family, computers have brought us closer together.

17. What TWO words are antonyms for the word "complex" used in paragraph 2 of "Calibrating Computers"?

(A) Easy

(B) Difficult

(C) Hard

(D) Simple

18. How is the story "Off To Camp" DIFFERENT from the article "Calibrating Computers"?

(A) The story is written in first-person, but the article is written in third-person.

(B) The story is fiction, but the article is factual.

(C) The story shows that life is better without computers, but the article explains why computers are necessary.

(D) The story is about true friendship, but the article is about fake, digital friendships.

19. How is the author's purpose for writing the story "Off To Camp" DIFFERENT from the author's purpose for writing the article "Calibrating Computers"?

(A) The purpose of the story is to entertain, but the purpose of the article is to give information.

(B) The purpose of the story is to explain real life friendship, but the purpose of the article is to explain digital friendships.

(C) The purpose of the story is to describe summer camp, but the purpose of the article is to describe the use of email.

(D) The purpose of the story is to show why computers are important, but the purpose of the article is to show why camp is important.

Read the selection and choose the best answer to each question.

(1) In a classroom filled with light so bright,
A teacher stands, her heart so light,
With knowledge, patience, and a smile so wide,
She guides her students like a loving guide.

(5) With chalk in hand and books in a row,
She helps young minds flourish and grow,
She teaches math and science, literature too,
All the things they need to learn and pursue.

(9) In the morning's early light, she waits,
For her students to come through the gates,
With backpacks heavy and hearts so keen,
To explore the world through the lessons unseen.

(13) She listens to stories, both big and small,
And answers questions, one and all,
With kindness in her heart and wisdom to share,
She shows her students that she truly cares.

(17) When challenges arise, and doubts creep in,
She tells them, "You can, and you will win,"
She builds their confidence, helps them believe,
That with hard work and dreams, they can achieve.

(21) With every lesson, she plants a seed,
Of knowledge and kindness, the tools they need,
To be brave and strong, to aim for the sky,
In her classroom, they learn to reach high.

(25) So, to the teachers who light up each day,
We thank you for showing us the way,
You're heroes of learning, and it's plain to see,
You make the world better, for you are the key.

20. The most likely reason the poet includes lines 1 through 8 in the poem is to—

(A) Help us to picture the teacher in her classroom ready to teach her students.

(B) Show us how difficult it is to become a teacher.

(C) Explain what the students will be having a test on in the next week.

(D) Describes the materials needed to be a student in her class.

21. The poet describes teachers being a "loving guide" in line 4 in order to show that—

(A) Teaching is a very hard job.

(B) Teachers love math and science.

(C) Teachers care about helping their students grow.

(D) School hours are usually Monday through Friday.

22. What does the word flourish mean in line 6?

(A) Annoy

(B) Decrease

(C) Solid

(D) Grow

23. Based on the tone of the poem, how does the author feel about teachers?

(A) They are amazing heroes.

(B) They are very underpaid.

(C) Teachers are very good at learning other languages.

(D) Most teachers are bored if they have to teach Math.

24. Why would a teacher need to have "chalk in hand"?

(A) She needs to use the chalk to take attendance.

(B) It helps her paint pictures for her students.

(C) They draw on the chalkboard to help teach her students.

(D) Chalk can come in many colors.

25. Read line 13 from the poem.

She listens to stories, both big and small,

This line shows that the teacher–

(A) Only listens to stories that include shapes and sizes.

(B) Appreciates all of her student's ideas and thoughts.

(C) Has her students write different stories for English class.

(D) Is writing a book on what it takes to become a teacher.

26. Notice the imagery used in line 9 from the poem.

In the morning's early light

This line symbolizes—

(A) Teaching hours are usually from 8am to 3pm.

(B) Teachers get to work very early in the morning to get ready for their day.

(C) The light in the morning is very faint and soft.

(D) Teachers should drive with their headlights on in the morning because it's still dark.

27. Read the poem again. Based on the details in the poem, write a response to the following:

Explain how the teacher feels about teaching their class of students. Write a well-organized essay from the perspective of the teacher. Use evidence from the poem to support the teacher's perspective.

Remember to:
- Clearly state your central idea
- Organize your writing
- Develop your ideas in detail
- Use evidence from the selection in your response
- Use correct spelling, capitalization, punctuation, and grammar.

Manage your time carefully so that you can:
- Review the selection
- Plan your response
- Write your response
- Revise and edit your response

18

_____

_____

_____

_____

_____

_____

_____

_____

_____

Read the selection and choose the best answer to each question. As you read the story, look for revisions that need to be made. Answer the questions that follow.

It was happening in Harmonyvile. So much excitement was around. The "Singing Star Contest," the most awaited event of the year for fifth-graders was coming up.

Daniel a passionate young singer dreamt of sharing his love for music with the world. He practiced tirelessly, choosing the perfect song, "The Song of Dreams," a heartfelt tune about believing in oneself.

On the contest day, the Harmonyville Community Center was packed. Nervous but determined, Daniel took the stage and sang his heart out. His performance left everyone spellbound, his voice filled with emotion and passion.

When Daniel finished, people clapped. The judges declared him the winner, and he received a prize package filled with musical instruments.

Daniel's story became an inspiration for Harmonyvill while reminding everyone to follow their dreams and also reminding them to share their passions. He became the "Musical Maestro" of the town, spreading the joy of music wherever he went, proving that dreams can come true when you sing from the heart.

28. Read the first paragraph again.

It was happening in Harmonyvile. So much excitement was around. The "Singing Star Contest," the most awaited event of the year for fifth-graders was coming up.

What sentence would be the BEST introduction for this story?

(A) The town was Harmonyville. The contest was "Singing Star Contest". And excitement was everywhere for the fifth-graders.

(B) It was happening in Harmonyvile. So much excitement was around. The "Singing Star Contest," the most awaited event of the year for fifth-graders was coming up.

(C) The "Singing Star Contest" was coming to Harmonuville. All fifth-graders were excited.

(D) In the lively neighborhood of Harmonyville, excitement buzzed around the "Singing Star Contest," the most awaited event of the year for fifth-graders.

29. Which sentence below is the corrected version of this sentence from the story:

Daniel a passionate young singer dreamt of sharing his love for music with the world.

(A) Daniel, a passionate young singer, dreamt of sharing his love for music with the world.

(B) Daniel–a passionate young singer–dreamt of sharing his love for music with the world.

(C) Daniel a passionate and young, singer dreamt of sharing his love for music with the world.

(D) Daniel a passionate young singer dreamt of sharing his love for music with the world.

30. What is the BEST way to revise this sentence?

When Daniel finished, people clapped.

(A) When Daniel finished, people clapped.

(B) When Daniel finished, the room erupted in applause.

(C) People were glad when Daniel finished.

(D) Daniel finished. People clapped.

31. This sentence needs to be revised. On the lines provided, rewrite the sentence in a clear and effective way.

Daniel's story became an inspiration for Harmonyvill while reminding everyone to follow their dreams and also reminding them to share their passions.

_____

_____

_____

_____

_____

Read the selection and choose the best answer to each question.

Jordan wrote this paper about flying. Read Jordan's paper and look for revisions she needs to make. Then answer the questions that follow.

Soaring High: A Guide to Flying on an Airplane

Introduction: Flying on an airplane is like embarking on an amazing adventure above the clouds. In this paper, we'll explore what it's like to fly, from preparing for your flight to enjoying the journey in the sky.

Getting Ready: Before you fly, make sure you have your ticket. Also identification (like a passport), and any necessary documents. Arrive at the airport with plenty of time to spare, so you don't feel rushed. Don't forget to pack your suitcase with the essentials!

Security Check: At the airport, you'll go through security. Be prepared to take off your shoes, place your belongings in a tray, and walk through a scanner. It's all about keeping everyone safe in the air.

Boarding: Once it's time to board, listen for your flight announcement. Follow the signs to your gate, and when your row is called, show your ticket to the flight attendants and walk down the jetway to the plane.

Takeoff and Landing: Buckle up! When you're on the plane, find your seat and fasten your seatbelt. During takeoff, the plane will speed up and lift off the ground, which can feel a bit like a roller coaster. Once in the air, it's smooth sailing. Before landing, the plane will descend, and you might feel a bit of pressure in your ears.

In-Flight Fun: While on the plane, you can watch movies, read books, or play games to pass the time. The flight attendants will serve food and drinks, so you won't go hungry. Don't forget to stay hydrated!

Enjoy the View: Look out the window to see beautiful landscapes from above the clouds. You might spot cities, mountains, or even other planes. It's like having a bird's-eye view of the world!

Arrival: When the plane lands, stay seated until it's your turn to exit. Follow the signs to baggage claim to collect your luggage. Now you've reached your destination!

Conclusion: Flying on an airplane is an exciting adventure that lets you travel to faraway places. By being prepared, staying safe, and enjoying the in-flight entertainment, you'll have an amazing time in the sky.

32. What would be the BEST transitional phrase between the Enjoy the View paragraph and the Arrival paragraph?

(A) Now, when the plane lands

(B) Then you land.

(C) Soon you will begin your descent.

(D) In conclusion

33. What is the MOST effective way to combine these two sentences from the Getting Ready section?

Before you fly, make sure you have your ticket. Also identification (like a passport), and any necessary documents.

(A) Before you fly, make sure you have your ticket, identification (such as passport), and any necessary documents.

(B) Before you fly, make sure you have your ticket. You also need identification, like a passport. Finally, you need any necessary documents.

(C) Before you fly, get identification, passport, documents.

(D) Get your identification (such as a passport) and any necessary documents, plus your ticket–all before you fly.

34. What does the word hydrated mean in the In-Flight Fun section?

(A) Hungry for food

(B) Starving for attention

(C) With enough water

(D) Quiet during the movies

35. Which sentence can BEST be added at the end of the Conclusion section to bring this paper to a more effective ending?

(A) So, fasten your seatbelt and get ready to soar high above the clouds!

(B) Flying is loads of fun if you come prepared!

(C) Maybe one day you'll be a pilot too!

(D) Remember, security is the most important thing to take into consideration!

Read the selection and choose the best answer to each question.

A student wrote the following paragraph. Look for corrections that need to be made. Then answer the questions that follow.

(1) Eagles are like big birds with sharp beaks and talons. (2) They live up high in the sky and make nests in trees. (3) Eagles fly around a lot and have good eyes for spoting stuff. (4) They eat things like fish and other animels. (5) Eagles are pretty strong and can grab things with their talons. (6) They make loud screechy sounds, and they're kinda like the kings of the bird world. (7) So, yeah, eagles are big, fly high, and eat animals with sharp beaks and claws. (8) Flying!

36. What is the BEST sentence to replace sentence (1)?

(A) Eagles–they are big birds. With sharp beaks and talons.

(B) Eagles are large birds with sharp beaks and talons.

(C) Like big birds, Eagles have sharp beaks and talons.

(D) With sharp beaks and talons, Eagles are like big birds.

37. Which word in sentence (3) is spelled incorrectly?
Eagles fly around a lot and have good eyes for spoting stuff.

(A) eagles

(B) around

(C) spoting

(D) stuff

38. Which option below is the BEST choice to replace sentence (7)?

(A) So, yeah, eagles are big, fly high, and eat animals with sharp beaks and claws.

(B) As you can see, eagles—they fly high, are big, eat animals, and have sharp features.

(C) Concluding with this: Eagles are big, fly high, eat animals, have sharp beaks and sharp claws.

(D) Eagles are amazing, with their sharp beaks and claws. They are huge, fly high, and eat other animals.

39. The correct spelling of animels from line (4) is—

(A) animals

(B) animels

(C) animles

(D) animuls

40. Sentence (8) is called what?

(A) Conclusion

(B) Run-on sentence

(C) Fragment

(D) Compound word

41. What is the correct way to write sentence (2)?

(A) Eagles soar high in the sky and even make nests in tall trees.

(B) No change is needed.

(C) They live up high in the sky and make nests in trees

(D) Eagles make high nests because they fly high in the sky.

42. What is the BEST title for this passage?

(A) Birds

(B) Flying in the Sky

(C) The Diet of Eagles

(D) The Amazing Eagle

Read the selection and choose the best answer to each question.

A student wrote the story below. Read the paragraph and look for corrections that need to be made. Then, answer the questions that follow.

(1) Once upon a time, there's a cat. (2) The cat was furry and had eyes. (3) Creepy. (4) It lived in a house, and the house had rooms and walls. (5) Cat slept all day long. (6) The cat walked around the house some times. (7) It meowed and ate fod.

43. Which is the BEST correction for sentence (1)?

(A) Once upon a time, there was a cat.

(B) Yikes–a creepy cat!

(C) There was a cat.

(D) Look–a cat.

44. Which is the BEST correction for sentence (2)?

(A) The cat was furry. It had eyes, of course.

(B) The cat was fury with eyes.

(C) The cat was furry and had pretty eyes.

(D) The cat had furry eyes.

45. Which is the BEST correction for sentence (3)?

A) Creepy!

B) May be the cat was creepy!

C) The cat was a little creepy.

D) The cat so creepy!

46. Which is the BEST correction for sentence (4)?

A) It lived in a house, and the house had rooms and walls.

B) It lived in a house that had rooms and walls.

C) It had rooms and walls and lived in a house.

D) It's house had rooms. It also had walls.

47. Which is the BEST correction for sentence (5)?

A) Cats sleep all day.

B) Cats sleeping all day long.

C) Cat slept all day long.

D) The cat slept all day long.

48. Which is the BEST correction for sentence (6)?

(A) The cat walked around the house some times.

(B) The cat walked around the house sometimes.

(C) Look–that cat is walking around the house!

(D) Some times, the cat walked around the house.

49. Which is the BEST correction for sentence (7)?

(A) It meowed and ate fud.

(B) It meowed and eats the food.

(C) It meowed and ate food.

(D) It meows.It eats food.

50. **Read the passage below. Rewrite the passage using correct spelling, grammar, and punctuation.**

Making your bed is like when you have to fix up your sleeping spot. Its boring and takes time away from more exciting things like playing video games. You have to straighten the blankets and pillows, and it's not fun. Sometimes, you wish you could just leave your bed all messy and not do any work. But grown-ups say you have to make your bed because it's important even if you'd rather be doing something else like eating cookies or watching cartoons. So, you do it, even though its not cool. The end.

Answers Test Practice 1

1. D, To teach the reader about the life of Abraham Lincoln
2. Written answer
3. B, Modest
4. A, The Emancipation Proclamation was incredibly important in the fight against slavery.
5. C, The bravery and courage Lincoln showed in his life lived on even today.
6. B, Abe believed that all people should be treated equally, no matter the color of their skin.
7. C, It summarizes the article and explains what the key points are to remember.
8. C, She is very excited to go to camp.
9. D, Teamwork and friendship are important in life.
10. B, Emma's mom and dad were worried about Emma being away at camp.
11. A, It sets up one of the adventures Emma and her new friends will have at camp.
12. C, Summer camp will happen again next year.
13. A, Process information quicker., B, Solve complex mathematical problems easily.
14. C, Computers can help make our daily lives easier.
15. D, It can be difficult to communicate with your friends in other countries.
16. B, This super-fast thinking is thanks to the tiny electronic brains inside them called microchips.
17. A, Easy, D, Simple
18. B, The story is fiction, but the article is factual.
19. A, The purpose of the story is to entertain, but the purpose of the article is to give information.
20. A, Help us to picture the teacher in her classroom ready to teach her students.
21. C, Teachers care about helping their students grow.
22. D, Grow
23. A, They are amazing heroes.
24. C, They draw on the chalkboard to help teach her students.
25. B, Appreciate all of her student's ideas and thoughts.
26. B, Teachers get to work very early in the morning to get ready for their day.
27. Written answer
28. D, In the lively neighborhood of Harmonyville, excitement buzzed around the "Singing Star Contest," the most awaited event of the year for fifth-graders.
29. A, Daniel, a passionate young singer, dreamt of sharing his love for music with the world.
30. B, When Daniel finished, the room erupted in applause.
31. Daniel's story served as an inspiration for Harmonyville, reminding everyone to pursue their dreams and share their passions.
32. C, Soon you will begin your descent.
33. A, Before you fly, make sure you have your ticket, identification (like a passport), and any necessary documents.
34. C, With enough water
35. A, So, fasten your seatbelt and get ready to soar high above the clouds!
36. B, Eagles are large birds with sharp beaks and talons.
37. C, spoting
38. D, Eagles are amazing, with their sharp beaks and claws. They are huge, fly high, and eat other animals.
39. A, animals
40. C, Fragment
41. A, Eagles soar high in the sky and even make nests in tall trees.
42. D, The Amazing Eagle
43. A, Once upon a time, there was a cat.
44. C, The cat was furry and had pretty eyes.
45. C, The cat was a little creepy.
46. B, It lived in a house that had rooms and walls.
47. D, The cat slept all day long.
48. B, The cat walked around the house sometimes.
49. C, It meowed and ate food.
50. Making your bed is like tidying up your sleeping area. It's boring and takes time away from more exciting activities, like playing video games. You have to straighten the blankets and pillows, and it's not fun. Sometimes, you wish you could leave your bed messy and avoid the work. But adults say you have to make your bed because it's important, even if you'd rather be doing something else, like eating cookies or watching cartoons. So, you do it, even though it's not cool. The end.

PRACTICE TEST 2

GET STARTED →

Read the following passage and answer the questions below.

(1) Once upon a time, there lived a man named Albert Einstein. He was a brilliant scientist who lived a long time ago and is still famous today for his amazing ideas.

(2) Albert was born in Germany in 1879. When he was a little boy, he was known for xbeing a bit different. He didn't speak until he was three years old, and his teachers thought he was slow in school. But Albert was actually really curious and loved to ask questions about how things worked.

(3) As Albert grew up, he developed a deep love for science and math. He would spend hours reading books and doing experiments in his spare time. He loved to imagine what it would be like to ride a beam of light!

(4) When Albert was a grown-up scientist, he came up with a famous theory called the Theory of Relativity. It explained how space and time are connected and how they are affected by things like gravity. His theory changed the way we understand the universe.

(5) In 1921, Albert Einstein won the Nobel Prize in Physics for his work on something called the "photoelectric effect." This discovery helped us understand how light works.

(6) Albert Einstein was a Jewish man, and during World War II, the Nazis came to power in Germany. They didn't like him because he was different, so he had to leave his home and move to the United States. There, he continued his important work.

(7) One of Albert's most famous equations is $E=mc^2$. It's a short formula that means a lot! It shows how energy (E) and mass (m) are related. This idea has been used to develop things like nuclear energy.

(8) Even though Albert Einstein passed away in 1955, his ideas continue to inspire scientists and thinkers all over the world. He showed us that it's okay to be different and that asking questions and using our imaginations can lead to incredible discoveries.

(9) Albert Einstein's life and work teach us that anyone, no matter where they come from or how different they may be, can make a big impact on the world with their curiosity and determination. So, remember, you can achieve amazing things too if you follow your passions and never stop asking questions!

1. What does the equation $E=mc^2$ represent, and why is it significant?

(A) It shows how energy and speed are related, and it has been used to develop faster airplanes.

(B) It shows how energy and mass are related, and it has been used to develop things like nuclear energy.

(C) It shows how energy and gravity are related, and it has been used to understand black holes.

(D) It shows how energy and light are related, and it has been used to create better light bulbs.

2. What is one reason the author presents the information in the article in chronological order? Support your answer with evidence from the article.

_____

_____

_____

_____

_____

_____

_____

_____

_____

_____

_____

3. What is most closely a synonym for the word "inspire" as used in paragraph 8?

(A) Motivate

(B) Dimminish

(C) Discourage

(D) Criticize

4. What is the key idea of paragraph 4?

(A) Einstein was a Jewish man who had to run from the Nazis.

(B) Einstein's teachers did not think he was a very intelligent boy.

(C) Photoelectric effect helps us understand how light works.

(D) The Theory of Relativity was an important scientific discovery.

5. Based on information in paragraph 2 and paragraph 3, the reader can conclude that–

(A) Einstein made amazing discoveries in the subject of Science.

(B) It is incredibly hard to win the Nobel Peace Prize.

(C) Though Einstein didn't talk early in his life, he was a very dedicated student.

(D) Einstein's scientific theories changed the universe as we know it.

6. Which sentence is used to support the idea that adults didn't think Albert was very smart?

(A) He didn't speak until he was three years old, and his teachers thought he was slow in school.

(B) So, remember, you can achieve amazing things too if you follow your passions and never stop asking questions!

(C) They didn't like him because he was different, so he had to leave his home and move to the United States.

(D) As Albert grew up, he developed a deep love for science and math.

7. Which paragraphs focus on Albert Einstein's significant scientific contributions and their impact?

- (A) Paragraphs 1 and 2
- (B) Paragraphs 3 and 4
- (C) Paragraphs 4 and 5
- (D) Paragraphs 1 and 6

Read the next two selections. Then choose the best answer to each question.

Cooking Up Fun

(1) Once upon a sunny summer morning, in a cozy kitchen filled with the inviting aroma of freshly baked bread, there was a fifth-grader named Ethan who was about to try something new – cooking classes. With an apron tied around his waist and a chef's hat perched atop his head, he arrived at Chef Maria's Culinary School, ready to explore the world of flavors.

(2) Chef Maria's Culinary School was a magical place, with colorful ingredients and laughter filling the air. The kitchen was equipped with shiny pots and pans, a rainbow of spices, and countertops just waiting to be transformed into culinary masterpieces.

(3) Ethan's first class was all about the basics – chopping, dicing, and slicing. He met his classmates, Lily, Alex, and Sofia, and they quickly became a culinary dream team. Together, they learned new skills in the kitchen, from whipping up fluffy pancakes for breakfast to crafting mouthwatering pizzas for lunch.

(4) One day, Chef Maria announced a cooking competition. The teams were chosen, and Ethan found himself on "Team Spice Masters" with his new friends. Their challenge was to create a delicious three-course meal using a secret ingredient – mangoes.

(5) As they brainstormed ideas, Ethan's heart raced with excitement. They decided to start with a mango salsa appetizer, followed by mango-glazed chicken, and finished with a refreshing mango sorbet. They practiced chopping mangoes, experimenting with flavors, and perfecting their dishes.

(6) The day of the competition arrived, and "Team Spice Masters" presented their meal to Chef Maria and the other students. The mango-themed dishes received rave reviews, and they won the competition. They celebrated their victory with a feast of their creations and shared their recipes with the class.

(7) As the weeks passed, Ethan learned valuable lessons about teamwork, creativity, and the joy of cooking. He discovered that the best part of cooking classes was not just the delicious food but the friendships he had forged along the way. And so, with a heart full of culinary knowledge and cherished memories, Ethan knew that Chef Maria's Culinary School would always hold a special place in his heart. He couldn't wait to return for more adventures in the kitchen and to share his passion for cooking with his family and friends.

Creative Colors

(1) Colors are like the paintbrushes of the world, adding beauty and vibrancy to everything around us. They come in an endless array of shades and tones, each with its own unique personality. Think of the colors you see every day – the blue of the sky, the green of grass, the red of a ripe apple, and the many hues of a rainbow.

(2) Colors have a special way of making our world feel alive and exciting. They can evoke emotions and feelings. For example, the color blue often makes people feel calm and peaceful, while the color red can make our hearts race with excitement. Artists use colors to create stunning paintings, and fashion designers use them to make clothes that express our style and personality.

(3) Colors are also a part of culture and tradition. In some cultures, certain colors have special meanings. For example, in many Asian cultures, red is a color of luck and happiness, often seen during celebrations and festivals. Colors can also help us navigate and understand our world. For instance, traffic lights use the colors red, yellow, and green to guide drivers safely.

(4) So, next time you look around, take a moment to appreciate the wonderful world of colors that surround you. They make our lives more beautiful, more interesting, and even more meaningful. Colors are like a magical palette that brings joy and inspiration to our world every day.

8. What is Ethan wearing when he arrives at Chef Maria's Culinary School?

(A) A chef's coat and gloves

(B) A chef's hat and an apron

(C) A sports uniform

(D) A painter's smock

9. What was Ethan's main lesson in "Cooking Up Fun"?

(A) Cooking can be very difficult.

(B) You can make a lot of money being a famous Chef.

(C) Making new friends can be just as much fun as cooking.

(D) Knowing how to properly prepare fruit is an important cooking skill.

10. Read paragraph 4 again from "Cooking Up Fun". Which sentence below would NOT fit well into this paragraph?

(4) One day, Chef Maria announced a cooking competition. The teams were chosen, and Ethan found himself on "Team Spice Masters" with his new friends. Their challenge was to create a delicious three-course meal using a secret ingredient – mangoes.

(A) Ethan hoped that the cooking lessons could continue for a long time to come.

(B) Ethan and his friends thought of every meal they knew that included mangoes.

(C) Ethan carefully began slicing up the mangoes.

(D) The secret ingredient was one Ethan had never even tried before!

11. How is paragraph 2 important to the plot of the story "Cooking Up Fun"?

(A) It introduces Ethan's new friends.

(B) It describes the conflict that Ethan and his friends will face.

(C) It sets the scene for the story.

(D) It summarizes the main idea of the story.

12. What does paragraph 7 in "Cooking Up Fun" tell us about what might happen next?

(A) Ethan will go back to school and finish the year strong.

(B) Ethan is ready for his big test in History class.

(C) Ethan doubts that he can become a chef later in life.

(D) Ethan will continue to cook for this family.

13. What are TWO things colors can do for us in the article "Creative Colors"?

(A) Evoke emotions.

(B) Help us get into a difficult Art school.

(C) Make our world more exciting.

(D) Help us prepare for a career in the military.

14. What is the central idea of the article "Creative Colors"?

(A) Colors can be boring and uninteresting.

(B) Some colors are ugly, while others are beautiful.

(C) We should appreciate the colors that are all around us.

(D) Colors can be blended with chalk and pastels.

15. Read paragraph 2 again from "Creative Colors". What is the author trying to explain to us?

(2) Colors have a special way of making our world feel alive and exciting. They can evoke emotions and feelings. For example, the color blue often makes people feel calm and peaceful, while the color red can make our hearts race with excitement. Artists use colors to create stunning paintings, and fashion designers use them to make clothes that express our style and personality.

(A) Colors can impact our emotions.

(B) Giving a painting to someone is a great way to show someone that you care.

(C) You need to be born with artistic talent to truly inspire beautiful artwork.

(D) Bright colors are the best colors for Art projects.

16. Which sentence gives us a specific example of color in our daily life in the article "Creative Colors"?

(A) So, next time you look around, take a moment to appreciate the wonderful world of colors that surround you.

(B) For instance, traffic lights use the colors red, yellow, and green to guide drivers safely.

(C) Colors are like the paintbrushes of the world, adding beauty and vibrancy to everything around us.

(D) They can evoke emotions and feelings.

17. What TWO words are antonyms for the word "calm" used in paragraph 2 of "Creative Colors"?

(A) Subtle

(B) Quiet

(C) Chaotic

(D) Crazy

18. How is the story "Cooking Up Fun" DIFFERENT from the article "Creative Colors"?

(A) The story is written in first-person, but the article is written in third-person.

(B) The story is entertainment, but the article wants to teach us to appreciate something.

(C) The story shows that cooking is better than painting.

(D) The story shows that being a chef is more practical than being an artist.

19. How are the authors SIMILAR in the story "Cooking Up Fun" and in the article "Creative Colors"?

(A) You can tell that both authors are excited about the subject matter.

(B) Both authors believe that cooking is a form of art.

(C) You can tell they are both from the same area of town.

(D) Each author wants you to live their story more than the other one.

Read the selection and choose the best answer to each question.

(1) On a football field bathed in golden light,
A coach stands tall, his heart so light,
With wisdom, patience, and a grin so wide,
He guides his team with unwavering pride.

(5) With whistle in hand and players in a row,
He helps young athletes improve and grow,
He teaches tactics, teamwork, strength, and more,
All the things they need for gridiron galore.

(9) In the morning's early light, he awaits,
For his players to storm through the gates,
With helmets, cleats, and hearts so keen,
To chase victories, on the grass so green.

(13) He listens to their stories, big and small,
And answers questions, giving his all,
With kindness in his heart and wisdom to spare,
He shows his team that he truly cares.

(17) When challenges arise and doubts take flight,
He tells them, "You can, and you'll shine bright,"
He builds their confidence, helps them believe,
With dedication and dreams, they will achieve.

(21) With every practice, he plants a seed,
Of discipline and teamwork, the tools they need,
To be brave on the field, aiming for the sky,
In his guidance, they learn to reach high.

(25) So, to the coaches who inspire each play,
We thank you for leading the way,
You're heroes of the game, it's plain to see,
You make the team better, for you are the key.

20. The most likely reason the poet includes lines 9 through 16 in the poem is to–

A) It shows how much you can be paid to coach football.

B) It helps us imagine the championship game and whether the team will win or lose.

C) It explains how a football team practices for the big game.

D) It gives us specific examples of what coaches do.

21. The poet describes coaches as having "unwavering pride" in line 4 in order to show that–

A) Most coaches are also teachers at their local school.

B) Coaches love teaching their team how to play.

C) All coaches used to play sports when they were kids.

D) It's better to be a football coach rather than a baseball coach.

22. What does the word storm mean in line 10?

(A) Run

(B) Rain

(C) Thunder

(D) Sleep

23. Based on the tone of the poem, how does the author feel about coaches?

(A) The author admires the leadership and pride of coaches.

(B) Coaches are often too hard on the players.

(C) If you are not talented, coaches will not try to help you get better.

(D) Coaches should be paid more for their work.

24. Why would the coach need to motivate his team?

(A) The players did not practice enough in the weight room.

(B) His team is certain they will win.

(C) The players might not think they are good enough to win.

(D) The team is excellent and doesn't need to practice anymore.

25. Read line 13 from the poem. *"They listen to their stories, big and small,"* This line shows that the coach–

(A) Only listens to the quarterback.

(B) Cares for all of his players, no matter what they might be sharing.

(C) Is not concerned with what the players are going through.

(D) Wants his team to write a book about all of their practices and game experiences.

44

26. Notice the imagery used in line 9 from the poem. *"In the morning's early light"*
This line symbolizes–

(A) Most coaches do not work at night.

(B) Since many coaches during the day, they can only practice in the morning.

(C) Football practice has to start at 7:00am

(D) The coach is ready to start working very early.

27. Read the poem again. Based on the details in the poem, write a response to the following:

Explain how the coach feels helping his players get better.

Write a well-organized essay from the perspective of the coach. Use evidence from the poem to support the coach's perspective.

Remember to:
- Clearly state your central idea
- Organize your writing
- Develop your ideas in detail
- Use evidence from the selection in your response
- Use correct spelling, capitalization, punctuation, and grammar.

Manage your time carefully so that you can:
- Review the selection
- Plan your response
- Write your response
- Revise and edit your response

_____

_____

_____

_____

_____

_____

_____

_____

_____

_____

_____

_____

_____

Read the selection and choose the best answer to each question. As you read the story, look for revisions that need to be made. Answer the questions that follow.

It happened in Petville. There was a big and fun contest called the "Get a Dog Competition." Fifth-graders had to write an essay explaining why they wanted a dog, with the best essay winning a new dog and a pet care package.

Emily, a girl who loved animals, entered the competition. She poured her heart into her essay, explaining how much joy and companionship a dog would bring to her life. Her dog would be amazing loving kind and helpful.

On the day of the competition, Emily read her heartfelt essay, touching the hearts of everyone in the room. The judges declared her the winner.
A few weeks later…Emily got her new furry friend–a playful puppy named Max. They became inseparable, sharing adventures and learning about responsibility.

Emily and Max's story inspired Petville and it was reminding everyone about the joy of pet ownership and also reminding them of the special bond between a child and their dog. They became known as the dynamic duo of Petville, spreading happiness wherever they went, showing that dreams can come true.

28. **Read the first paragraph again.**

It happened in Petville. There was a big and fun contest called the "Get a Dog Competition." Fifth-graders had to write an essay explaining why they wanted a dog, with the best essay winning a new dog and a pet care package.

What sentence would be the BEST introduction for this story?

- (A) In Petville there was a competition.
- (B) In the town of Petville, there was an exciting contest called the "Get a Dog Competition."
- (C) A contest started in Petville. It was called "Get a Dog Competition."
- (D) The town was Petville and the contest was called "Get a Dog Competition."

29. Which sentence below is the corrected version of this sentence from the story: *Her dog would be amazing loving kind and helpful.*

- (A) Her dog would be amazing and loving and kind and helpful.
- (B) Her dog would be amazing. Also loving, kind and helpful.
- (C) Her dog would be the following: amazing, loving, kind, and helpful.
- (D) Her dog would be amazing, loving, kind, and helpful.

30. What is the BEST way to revise this sentence?
A few weeks later…Emily got her new furry friend–a playful puppy named Max.

(A) A few weeks later, Emilly got her new furry friend, a playful puppy named Max.

(B) A few weeks later…Emily got her new furry friend…a playful puppy named Max.

(C) A few weeks later Emily got her new furry friend. It was Max, a playful puppy.

(D) Emily got her new furry friend. A playful puppy named Max. It was a few weeks later.

31. This sentence needs to be revised. On the lines provided, rewrite the sentence in a clear and effective way.

Emily and Max's story inspired Petville and it was reminding everyone about the joy of pet ownership and also reminding them of the special bond between a child and their dog.

_____

_____

_____

_____

_____

_____

Read the selection and choose the best answer to each question.

Elijah wrote this paper about baseball. Read Elijah's paper and look for revisions he needs to make. Then answer the questions that follow.

A Home Run Guide to Learning Baseball

Introduction: Learning to play baseball is a fantastic adventure filled with excitement and teamwork. In this paper, we'll explore the basics of playing baseball, from getting started to hitting home runs!

48

Getting Started: The first step in learning baseball is to gather your gear. You'll need a baseball glove that fits your hand. Plus comfortable sports shoes or cleats, and a baseball bat. Don't forget to wear a baseball cap to protect your eyes from the sun!

Learn the Basics: Baseball has some important positions, like pitcher, catcher, and outfielder. Talk to your coach or experienced players to understand each role. Pay attention to the rules of the game, like how to run bases and how to score points (called runs).

Practice, Practice, Practice: Practice makes perfect! Spend time practicing throwing and catching with your teammates. Hone your batting skills by swinging at pitches or hitting off a tee. The more you practice, the better you'll get.

Teamwork: Baseball is a team sport, so working together is crucial. Communicate with your teammates, cheer each other on, and always be supportive. Remember, there's no "I" in "team"!

Baseball Drills: Drills are like exercises that help you improve specific baseball skills. Work on your throwing accuracy, running speed, and catching ability with fun drills. It's like training to become a baseball superstar!

Stay Safe: Safety is super important in baseball. Wear your helmet when batting, and pay attention to your coach's safety instructions. Protect yourself from the sun with sunscreen and stay hydrated during hot games.

Game Day: On game day, wear your team uniform with pride. Be respectful to the coaches, referees, and opposing players. Remember, winning is great, but sportsmanship is even more important.

Have Fun: The most important thing is to have fun! Whether you win or lose, playing baseball should make you smile. Enjoy the fresh air, the sound of the crowd, and the thrill of the game.

Conclusion: Learning to play baseball is an exciting journey that teaches you teamwork, sportsmanship, and valuable life skills. With the right gear, practice, and a positive attitude, you'll be hitting home runs and having a blast on the baseball field in no time.

32. What would be the BEST transitional phrase between the Stay Safe paragraph and the Game Day paragraph?

(A) Now, on game day

(B) In conclusion

(C) For example

(D) In addition to staying safe, you'll need to wear your uniform

33. What is the MOST effective way to combine these two sentences from the Getting Started section?

You'll need a baseball glove that fits your hand. Plus comfortable sports shoes or cleats, and a baseball bat.

A You'll need a baseball glove that fits your hand, comfortable sports shoes or cleats, and a baseball bat.

B You'll need a baseball glove that fits your hand. Plus comfortable sports shoes or cleats. Also a baseball bat.

C You'll need: a baseball glove that fits your hand…comfortable sports shoes or cleats…and a baseball bat.

D You'll need the following: 1. a baseball glove that fits your hand 2. comfortable sports shoes or cleats 3. baseball bat.

34. What does the word hydrated mean in the Stay Safe section?

A Hungry for food

B Starving for attention

C With enough water

D Warmed up for running

35. Which sentence can BEST be added at the end of the Conclusion section to bring this paper to a more effective ending?

A If your team wins, then you'll know you came prepared!

B So, step up to the plate, and let the baseball adventure begin!

C Don't forget cleats in order to not hurt yourself on the field!

D And always remember your equipment for every game!

Read the selection and choose the best answer to each question.

A student wrote the following paragraph. Look for corrections that need to be made. Then answer the questions that follow.

(1) Anteaters are like weird bug-loving animals with long noses and stuff. (2) They live in far places and eat ants and termites with their tongues, which are long, I guess. (3) They look kinda shaggy and slow and have big claws for diging and stuff. (4) They don't talk much and do their own thing. (5) So, anteaters are these strang creatures with long noses and tongues, and they really like ants and termites. (6) I saw one at the zoo it was really interesting and kind of weird at the same time.

36. What is the BEST sentence to replace sentence (1)?

(A) Anteaters. They are weird animals that just love bugs.

(B) Anteaters are bug-loving animals with unique features.

(C) Anteaters have long noses. This is because they love to eat bugs. So they need it to find them in long holes.

(D) Let's talk about anteaters, which love to eat bugs, and have long noses.

37. Which word in sentence (3) is spelled incorrectly?
They look kinda shaggy and slow and have big claws for diging and stuff.

(A) diging

(B) shaggy

(C) claws

(D) stuff

38. Which option below is the BEST choice to replace sentence (5)?

(A) So, anteaters are these strange creatures with long noses and tongues, and they really like ants and termites.

(B) Concluding–anteaters are strange creatures with long noses and tongues. They really like ants and termites and other bugs.

(C) Anteaters are unique creatures with long noses and tongues. They are helpful to our environment since they eat bugs like ants and termites.

(D) Want an anteater? Just remember that they have long noses and tongues and need to eat ants and termites!

39. The correct spelling of strang from line (5) is–

(A) strang

(B) strange

(C) straying

(D) stranche

40. Sentence (6) is called what?

(A) Fragment

(B) Run-on sentence

(C) Conclusion

(D) Compound word

41. What is the correct way to write sentence (2)?

(A) They live in far places and eat ants and termites with their tongues, which are long, I guess.

(B) Anteaters live in far off places. They must have long tongues in order to be able to eat ants and termites.

(C) Living in far places, anteaters eat ants termites with, I guess, long tongues.

(D) No change is needed.

52

42. What is the BEST title for this passage?

(A) Termites and Other Pests

(B) Animals with Long Tongues

(C) Amazing Antelopes!

(D) The Wonderful Anteaters

Read the selection and choose the best answer to each question.
A student wrote the story below. Read the paragraph and look for corrections that need to be made. Then answer the questions that follow.

(1) There was dog. (2) It was brown and had furr. (3) The dog living in a place with a yard. (4) It runs in the yard. (5) It barked some times. (6) The dog ate food frum a bowl. (7) It liked to sleeping.

43. Which is the BEST correction for sentence (1)?

(A) There was dog.

(B) Look–dogs!

(C) Once upon a time there was a dog.

(D) There were dogs.

44. Which is the BEST correction for sentence (2)?

(A) It was furry and brown.

(B) It was brown. It had fur.

(C) It's furr was brown.

(D) Brown and furry–that's how I'd describe the dog.

53

45. Which is the BEST correction for sentence (3)?

(A) The dog–living in a place with a yard.

(B) The dog is living, but it has a yard!

(C) The dog lived in a place with a yard.

(D) It's got a yard–the place where the dog lived.

46. Which is the BEST correction for sentence (4)?

(A) It runs in the yard.

(B) It ran in the yard.

(C) It's running all allong the yard.

(D) It runned in the yard.

47. Which is the BEST correction for sentence (5)?

(A) It barked sometimes.

(B) Some times, it barked.

(C) It barked some times.

(D) It barked allways.

48. Which is the BEST correction for sentence (6)?

(A) The dog ate food frum a bowl?

(B) The dog eates from bowls.

(C) The dog is eating frum a bowl!

(D) The dog ate from a bowl.

54

49. Which is the BEST correction for sentence (7)?

(A) It liked sleeps.

(B) It liked sleeping alot.

(C) It liked to sleep.

(D) Likes sleeping? Oh yes!

50. **Read the passage below. Rewrite the passage using correct spelling, grammar, and punctuation.**

Reign is like when watter falz from the sky. It's wet and makes everything dammp. You have to use an umbrella or where a coat, and that's not fun. Sometimes, it messes up yor plans to go outside and play. You wish it would stop rainin' so you could do fun stuff instead. But, rain just keeps comin down, and it's not nike at all.

_____

_____

_____

_____

_____

_____

_____

_____

_____

_____

_____

Answers Test Practice 2

1. B, It shows how energy and mass are related, and it has been used to develop things like nuclear energy.
2. Written answer
3. A, Motivate
4. D, The Theory of Relativity was an important scientific discovery.
5. C, Though Einstein didn't talk early in his life, he was a very dedicated student.
6. A, He didn't speak until he was three years old, and his teachers thought he was slow in school.
7. C, Paragraphs 4 and 5
8. B, A chef's hat and an apron
9. C, Making new friends can be just as much fun as cooking.
10. A, Ethan hoped that the cooking lessons could continue for a long time to come.
11. C, It sets the scene for the story.
12. D, Ethan will continue to cook for this family.
13. A, Evoke emotions., C, Make our world more exciting.
14. C, We should appreciate the colors that are all around us.
15. A, Colors can impact our emotions.
16. B, For instance, traffic lights use the colors red, yellow, and green to guide drivers safely.
17. C, Chaotic, D, Crazy
18. B, The story is entertainment, but the article wants to teach us to appreciate something.
19. A, You can tell that both authors are excited about the subject matter.
20. D, It gives us specific examples of what coaches do.
21. B, Coaches love teaching their team how to play.
22. A, Run
23. A, The author admires the leadership and pride of coaches.
24. C, The players might not think they are good enough to win.
25. B, Cares for all of his players, no matter what they might be sharing.
26. D, The coach is ready to start working very early.
27. Written answer
28. B, In the town of Petville, there was an exciting contest called the "Get a Dog Competition."
29. D, Her dog would be amazing, loving, kind, and helpful.
30. A, A few weeks later, Emilly got her new furry friend, a playful puppy named Max.
31. Emily and Max's story served as an inspiration for Petville, reminding everyone of the delight of pet ownership and the unique bond between a child and their dog.
32. D, In addition to staying safe, you'll need to wear your uniform
33. A, You'll need a baseball glove that fits your hand, comfortable sports shoes or cleats, and a baseball bat.
34. C, With enough water
35. B, So, step up to the plate, and let the baseball adventure begin!
36. B, Anteaters are bug-loving animals with unique features.
37. A, diging
38. C, Anteaters are unique creatures with long noses and tongues. They are helpful to our environment since they eat bugs like ants and termites.
39. B, strange
40. B, Run-on sentence
41. B, Anteaters live in far off places. They must have long tongues in order to be able to eat ants and termites.
42. D, The Wonderful Anteaters
43. C, Once upon a time there was a dog.
44. A, It was furry and brown.
45. C, The dog lived in a place with a yard.
46. B, It ran in the yard.
47. A, It barked sometimes.
48. D, The dog ate from a bowl.
49. C, It liked to sleep.
50. Rain is when water falls from the sky. It's wet and makes everything damp. You have to use an umbrella or wear a coat, and that's not fun. Sometimes, it messes up your plans to go outside and play. You wish it would stop raining so you could do fun stuff instead. But, the rain just keeps coming down, and it's not nice at all.

PRACTICE TEST 3

GET STARTED →

Read the following passage and answer the questions below.

(1) Once upon a time, in the early 20th century, there was an extraordinary woman named Amelia Earhart. She was a fearless aviator who loved to fly high above the clouds. Amelia was born in 1897 in Atchison, Kansas, and from the moment she saw her first airplane, she was hooked.

(2) Amelia's dreams of flying took off when she took her first plane ride. From that moment on, she knew she wanted to be a pilot. She worked hard to save money for flying lessons and became the 16th woman in the world to earn her pilot's license.

(3) Amelia Earhart was determined to break records and show the world that women could be just as brave as men in the sky. In 1932, she made history by becoming the first woman to fly solo across the Atlantic Ocean. Imagine being all alone in the plane, surrounded by nothing but the vast ocean!

(4) But her adventures didn't stop there. In 1935, Amelia set yet another record by flying solo from Hawaii to California. She was a true trailblazer, proving that gender should never hold anyone back from pursuing their dreams.

(5) One of her most daring missions was an attempt to fly all the way around the world. On June 1, 1937, she and her navigator, Fred Noonan, started this incredible adventure. They traveled to many faraway places, but sadly, their plane disappeared somewhere over the Pacific Ocean. Despite extensive searches, they were never found, and the mystery of their disappearance remains unsolved to this day.

(6) Amelia Earhart's bravery and determination continue to inspire people of all ages. She taught us that it's essential to chase our dreams, no matter how big they may seem. Even though her last adventure ended in mystery, her legacy lives on, reminding us to be fearless and reach for the skies, just like Amelia did. Amelia Earhart will always be remembered as a symbol of courage, adventure, and the power of following your dreams.

1. What is the tone of the passage?

(A) Humorous and light-hearted

(B) Inspirational and admiring

(C) Sarcastic and critical

(D) Melancholic and somber

2. What is one reason the author presents the information in the article in chronological order? Support your answer with evidence from the article.

_____

_____

_____

_____

_____

_____

_____

_____

_____

_____

_____

_____

_____

3. What is most closely a synonym for the word "trailblazer" as used in paragraph 4?

(A) Leader

(B) Follower

(C) Investor

(D) Pilot

4. What is the key idea of paragraph 5?

(A) Earhart flew from Hawaii to California.

(B) Earhart was born in Kansas in 1897.

(C) The mystery of her final flight.

(D) Her legacy and courage live on even today.

5. Based on information found in paragraph 3 and paragraph 4, the reader can conclude that–

(A) Airplanes in the 1800s were not made to fly across the world.

(B) Earhart set many records during her lifetime.

(C) No one knows what happened to Earhart and her partner.

(D) Recently, people believed they may have found Earhart's crashed airplane.

6. Which sentence is used to support the idea that women shouldn't be looked down upon because they are female?

(A) She was a true trailblazer, proving that gender should never hold anyone back from pursuing their dreams.

(B) Even though her last adventure ended in mystery, her legacy lives on, reminding us to be fearless and reach for the skies, just like Amelia did.

(C) She was a fearless aviator who loved to fly high above the clouds.

(D) Amelia Earhart will always be remembered as a symbol of courage, adventure, and the power of following your dreams.

7. How does the author emphasize Amelia Earhart's achievements in the passage?

- (A) By comparing her to other male pilots
- (B) By listing her records and daring missions
- (C) By describing her physical appearance
- (D) By including dialogue from her speeches

Read the next two selections. Then choose the best answer to each question.

Spectacular Space

(1) Once upon a time, in the not-so-distant future, there was a girl named Mia who had an extraordinary dream – to travel to space. Her dream was about to come true as she stood in front of the spaceship launchpad, ready for the adventure of a lifetime.

(2) The spaceship, named "Stellar Voyager," was a marvel of modern technology. It gleamed in the sunlight, its sleek design ready to carry Mia and her fellow space travelers into the unknown. Mia, wearing her astronaut suit and helmet, felt a mix of excitement and wonder as she boarded the spacecraft.

(3) Inside, the spaceship was filled with blinking control panels, cozy sleeping pods, and giant windows that offered breathtaking views of the stars. Mia's fellow space travelers included scientists, engineers, and even a famous astronaut who had been to space before. They were like a big space family, all working together to explore the cosmos.

(5) Over the next few days, Mia and her fellow astronauts conducted exciting experiments, observed distant planets through telescopes, and marveled at the beauty of Earth from space. They even enjoyed space food, which was surprisingly tasty. Mia learned about the vastness of the universe, the importance of protecting our planet, and the thrill of discovery.

(6) One night, as Mia gazed out of the spaceship window, she saw a meteor shower lighting up the dark space. It was a breathtaking sight, and she couldn't help but feel a deep sense of awe and gratitude for the opportunity to be among the stars.

(7) As the mission came to an end, the spaceship began its journey back to Earth. Mia knew that this adventure would stay with her forever, and she was filled with a newfound passion for space exploration. She couldn't wait to share her experiences with her friends and family back on Earth.

(8) When the spaceship touched down safely, Mia stepped out onto solid ground with a heart full of wonder. Her trip to space had not only fulfilled her childhood dream but had also ignited a lifelong love for the cosmos. Mia knew that, just like the stars in the sky, her dreams were boundless, and she was ready to reach for them, one adventure at a time.

Sassy Squirrels

(1) Squirrels are some of the cutest and most energetic creatures you can find in your local park or even in your own backyard. These small mammals are known for their fluffy tails, sharp claws, and love for climbing trees. Squirrels come in different types, but the ones we often see are the gray squirrels and the reddish-brown ones called red squirrels.

(2) One of the most remarkable things about squirrels is their incredible agility. They can leap from branch to branch with ease and scamper up and down trees in the blink of an eye. Their sharp claws and strong legs help them do these amazing acrobatics. Squirrels are also famous for their love of nuts. In the fall, they busily collect acorns, walnuts, and other nuts to store for the winter. They dig little holes in the ground, bury the nuts, and remember where they put them, which is a clever trick!

(3) Another fun fact about squirrels is their chattering and chittering sounds. They use these noises to communicate with each other, often warning fellow squirrels about potential dangers like predators. Squirrels are quite social creatures and can often be seen playing or chasing each other in the treetops. So, the next time you spot a squirrel in your neighborhood, take a moment to enjoy their playful antics and appreciate their unique place in the natural world

8. What narrative technique does the author use to introduce the story in the first paragraph?

(A) Flashback

(B) Flash-forward

(C) In media res

(D) Dialogue

9. What was Mia's main lesson in "Spectacular Space"?

(A) Dreams really can come true.

(B) Training to be an astronaut was too difficult to accomplish.

(C) Dreams can be unrealistic.

(D) Friendship is the most important thing of all.

10. How does the author create a sense of camaraderie among Mia and her fellow space travelers in paragraph 3?

(A) By highlighting their shared goal and teamwork

(B) By describing their diverse backgrounds

(C) By detailing their individual accomplishments

(D) By showing them engaging in conflicts

11. How is paragraph 4 important to the plot of the story "Spectacular Space"?

(A) It explains the setting of the planets.

(B) It introduces the new characters of the story.

(C) It is the beginning of the conflict to the story.

(D) It is the beginning of the space flight.

12. Which sentence best illustrates the use of vivid imagery in the text?

(A) "Mia knew that this adventure would stay with her forever, and she was filled with a newfound passion for space exploration."

(B) "The spaceship, named 'Stellar Voyager,' was a marvel of modern technology."

(C) "One night, as Mia gazed out of the spaceship window, she saw a meteor shower lighting up the dark space."

(D) "They even enjoyed space food, which was surprisingly tasty."

13. What are TWO reasons the author gives for why squirrels are remarkable in the article "Sassy Squirrels"?

(A) They remember where they plant their nuts.

(B) They are very fluffy.

(C) They build very large nests.

(D) They are very agile.

14. What is the central idea of the article "Sassy Squirrels"?

(A) Squirrels are pests that can ruin our homes.

(B) Squirrels can jump very far distances.

(C) Squirrels can come in many varieties.

(D) We should appreciate the uniqueness of squirrels.

64

15. Read paragraph 3 again from "Sassy Squirrels". How are squirrels similar to human beings?

(3) Another fun fact about squirrels is their chattering and chittering sounds. They use these noises to communicate with each other, often warning fellow squirrels about potential dangers like predators. Squirrels are quite social creatures and can often be seen playing or chasing each other in the treetops. So, the next time you spot a squirrel in your neighborhood, take a moment to enjoy their playful antics and appreciate their unique place in the natural world.

(A) They can speak English.

(B) They communicate with each other.

(C) They can jump from tree to tree.

(D) They store acorns for the winter.

16. The very first sentence of paragraph 1 in "Sassy Squirrels" starts us off with what?

(A) An opinion.

(B) Factual information.

(C) Statistical data.

(D) An angry argument.

17. What TWO words are antonyms for the word "scamper" used in paragraph 2 in the article "Sassy Squirrels"?

(A) Run

(B) Scurry

(C) Sleep

(D) Sit

18. How is the story "Spectacular Space" DIFFERENT from the article "Sassy Squirrels"?

(A) The story is written in first-person, but the article is written in third-person.

(B) The story is about nature, but the article is about Science.

(C) The story is fiction, but the article is giving information.

(D) The story gives statistical information about planets, while the article gives statistical information about squirrels.

19. How is the author's purpose for writing the story "Spectacular Space" DIFFERENT from the author's purpose for writing the article "Sassy Squirrels"?

(A) The purpose of the story is to entertain, but the purpose of the article is to give information.

(B) The purpose of the story is to further explain mathematics, while the article is trying to explain the animal kingdom.

(C) The purpose of the story is to describe space, but the purpose of the article is to describe the geography.

(D) The purpose of the story is to show why space is important, but the purpose of the article is to show why trees are important.

Read the selection and choose the best answer to each question.

(1) In a kitchen filled with warmth so bright,
A chef stands tall, their heart so light,
With culinary skills and a grin so wide,
They create delicious dishes, a flavorful ride.

(5) With apron tied and ingredients in a row,
They craft gourmet wonders, watch flavors flow,
They mix and stir, bake, roast, and stew,
Cooking up delights for me and you.

(9) In the morning's early light, they rise,
To prepare scrumptious breakfasts, a delightful surprise,
With pots and pans and hearts so keen,
They turn simple ingredients into a taste machine.

66

(13) They listen to our cravings, big and small,
And serve us meals that satisfy us all,
With passion in their hearts and flavors to share,
They show us that in food, they genuinely care.

(17) When challenges arise, and a recipe seems tough,
They say, "Keep trying; you'll soon have enough,"
They build our confidence, help us believe,
That with practice and patience, we can achieve.

(21) With every dish, they plant a culinary seed,
Of creativity and flavors, the recipes we need,
To savor new tastes, to explore and try,
In their kitchen, we learn to reach for the sky.

(25) So, to the chefs who bring joy every day,
We thank you for cooking the food in a magical way,
You're the heroes of flavors, it's plain to see,
You make our meals better, for you are the key.

20. Which literary device is predominantly used throughout the poem to create rhythm and flow?

(A) Alliteration

(B) Rhyme

(C) Onomatopoeia

(D) Free verse

21. The poet describes dishes as being a "flavorful ride" in line 4 in order to show that–

(A) The meals are very hard to create.

(B) Being a chef takes many years of schooling and practice.

(C) Chefs are also excellent drivers.

(D) The meals are very tasty.

22. What does the word savor mean in line 23?

(A) Enjoy

(B) Ignore

(C) Annoy

(D) Distract

23. Based on the tone of the poem, how does the author feel about chefs?

(A) The author feels that it's an unimportant job.

(B) It's very expensive to go to culinary school.

(C) He greatly appreciates their hard work.

(D) If a chef doesn't follow the recipe correctly, the food will be very bad.

24. Why would a chef need to tie an apron on?

(A) Aprons are very pretty.

(B) Aprons protect their clothes from mess.

(C) If you are a chef, it's required that you have an apron.

(D) Aprons can say the chef's company name on it, which is good marketing.

25. Read line 13 from the poem. *They listen to our cravings, big and small,* This line shows that chefs—

(A) Only like to prepare desserts because they are very tasty.

(B) It's bad to have cravings if you are craving something unhealthy.

(C) A chef listens to what everyone wants.

(D) We should eat smaller, simpler portions.

26. What stylistic feature is used in the final stanza to emphasize the poem's message?

(A) Chefs wake up very early to get started cooking.

(B) Chefs prefer to make breakfast, as opposed to lunch or dinner.

(C) Chefs do not work at night.

(D) You need a lot of light in your kitchen to cook or bake.

27. Read the poem again. Based on the details in the poem, write a response to the following:

Explain how chefs feel about their job to prepare meals for people.

Write a well-organized essay from the perspective of the chef. Use evidence from the poem to support the chef's perspective.

Remember to:
- Clearly state your central idea
- Organize your writing
- Develop your ideas in detail
- Use evidence from the selection in your response
- Use correct spelling, capitalization, punctuation, and grammar.

Manage your time carefully so that you can:
- Review the selection
- Plan your response
- Write your response
- Revise and edit your response

_____

_____

_____

_____

_____

_____

_____

Read the selection and choose the best answer to each question. As you read the story, look for revisions that need to be made. Answer the questions that follow.

In the cozy town of Harvestville, there lived a boy named Juan who had a special love for two things: growing pumpkins and, unsurprisingly, carving them into fantastic works of art. Juan was well-known throughout the town for his extraordinary pumpkin creations, which he carefully crafted in his family's charming pumpkin patch. But there was one event in Harvestville that filled his heart with excitement every fall – the Great Harvestville Pumpkin Carving Contest.

The contest was the highlight of Harvestville's annual Autumn Festival, a celebration of all things related to the season. The festival featured pumpkin picking apple bobbing and scarecrow-building contests. It was a day filled with laughter, music, and, of course, pumpkins of all shapes and sizes.

Juan, having never entered the pumpkin carving contest before, was for certain that this year would be different. He felt an irresistible urge to prove his love for pumpkins and make his mark on Harvestville's history. With his carving tools in hand and a determined spark in his eye, Juan decided to sign up.

The day of the contest arrived, and the town square buzzed with excitement. There were pumpkins of every size and hue lined up on tables, ready to be transformed into art. Juan's eyes were drawn to the grand stage where the pumpkin carving contest would take place. There, under a canopy of colorful leaves, was a long table adorned with pumpkins, each one more enticing than the last.

Juan joined the other contestants, a mix of kids and adults, each with their own carving technique. Some had practiced for weeks, honing their skills, while others relied on their natural talent. Juan, however, drew inspiration from the pumpkins themselves and a secret plan – his unique "Harvestville Surprise" pumpkin carving, complete with intricate patterns and a surprise hidden inside.

As the contest kicked off and the timer started, and everyone began their creative work. Pumpkin pieces flew through the air, and the crowd cheered with every masterpiece that emerged. Juan, however, savored each stroke of his carving knife, finding joy in every twist and turn.

Minutes passed, and the group of contestants slowly dwindled. Juan found himself still going strong, feeling the artistic spirit flow through him. He knew he couldn't let Harvestville down. With the final "Harvestville Surprise" pumpkin before him, he took a deep breath and carved with all his might.

The crowd watched in wonder as Juan unveiled his last creation, revealing the hidden surprise within. Cheers erupted, and the judges declared him the winner of the Great Harvestville Pumpkin Carving Contest! Juan had not only conquered the contest but had also won the admiration of his town.

Juan realized his passion for pumpkins led him to victory and so he was very proud and had a big smile. He celebrated with his friends and family, knowing that this artistic triumph would be a cherished memory in Harvestville for years to come. From that day forward, Juan became known as the "Pumpkin Maestro" of Harvestville, and his love for pumpkins continued to bring joy to the town he adored.

28. This sentence needs to be revised. Which sentence below is the BEST revision?

Juan, having never entered the pumpkin carving contest before, was for certain that this year would be different.

(A) Juan had never entered a contest before. This would be largely different.

(B) This year would be different since Juan had never entered the pumpkin carving contest before.

(C) Juan had never entered the pumpkin carving contest before, but this year was different.

(D) Since Juan never entered the pumpkin carving contest before, and since he wanted this year to be different, Juan entered it.

29. Which sentence below is the corrected version of this sentence from the story:

The festival featured pumpkin picking apple bobbing and scarecrow-building contests.

(A) The festival featured pumpkin picking, apple bobbing, and scarecrow-building contests.

(B) The festival featured pumpkin, picking, apple, bobbing, and scarecrow-building contests.

(C) The festival featured; pumpkin picking apple bobbing and scarecrow-building contests?

(D) The festival featured pumpkin picking. And apple bobbing and scarecrow-building contests.

72

30. What is the BEST way to revise this sentence?

As the contest kicked off and the timer started, and everyone began their creative work.

(A) The contest kicked off. The timer started. Everyone began their creative work.

(B) Once the contest kicked off, everyone began their creative work. The timer started.

(C) As the contest kicked off and the timer started, and everyone began their creative work.

(D) As the contest kicked off, the timer started, and everyone began their creative work.

31. This sentence needs to be revised. On the lines provided, rewrite the sentence in a clear and effective way.

Juan realized his passion for pumpkins led him to victory and so he was very proud and had a big smile.

_____

_____

_____

_____

Read the selection and choose the best answer to each question.
Kim wrote this paper about babysitting. Read Kim's paper and look for revisions she needs to make. Then answer the questions that follow.

The Ultimate Guide to Babysitting Like a Pro

Introduction: Babysitting is an exciting and responsible job that many young people can do. In this paper, we'll explore how to be a fantastic babysitter and ensure the children you watch over have a great time while staying safe.
Prepare for Babysitting: Before you start babysitting, it's important to be prepared. Make sure you know the family's contact information, any emergency numbers, and the children's allergies or special needs. Always ask the parents about bedtime routines, favorite games, and any rules they want you to follow.

Safety First: Safety is the number one rule of babysitting. Keep an eye on the children at all times, especially if they're playing outside or near water. If you need to leave the room for any reason, make sure the children are safe and can't get into trouble. Lock away any harmful items like cleaning supplies or sharp objects.

Fun and Games: Kids love to have fun! Play games, read books, do arts and crafts, or have a dance party. Make sure to ask the kids what activities they enjoy and join in on the fun.

Feeding Time: If the parents haven't prepared meals or snacks, make sure to feed the children at the right times. Ask about any food allergies or preferences. Remember to keep the kitchen clean and put away any sharp utensils or hot appliances.

Bedtime Routine: Bedtime can be a bit tricky sometimes, but it's important for kids to get a good night's sleep. Follow the parents' instructions for bedtime routines. Things like brushing teeth, reading a story, or singing a lullaby. Make sure the kids are safe and comfy in their beds.

Dealing with Problems: Sometimes, kids might get upset or have disagreements. Stay calm and try to solve problems with kindness and patience. If you're unsure how to handle a situation, don't hesitate to call the parents for guidance.

Emergency Plans: Know what to do in case of emergencies. Have a list of important phone numbers, like the parents' contact information, a neighbor, or 911. Be familiar with basic first aid, and have a first aid kit handy.

Conclusion: Babysitting is a fun and rewarding job, but it also comes with responsibilities. Being prepared, keeping kids safe, having fun, and following the parents' instructions are all important aspects of babysitting.

32. What is the primary purpose of the introduction in this text?

(A) To tell a story about babysitting

(B) To introduce the topic and outline what will be covered

(C) To criticize bad babysitters

(D) To describe the author's personal experience with babysitting

33. What is the MOST effective way to combine these two sentences from the Bedtime Routine section?

Follow the parents' instructions for bedtime routines. Things like brushing teeth, reading a story, or singing a lullaby.

A. Follow the parents' instructions for bedtime routines, brushing teeth, reading a story, or singing a lullaby, and things like that.

B. Follow the parents' instructions for bedtime routines. Things like brushing teeth, reading a story, or singing a lullaby.

C. Follow the parents' instructions for bedtime routines, maybe with ideas such as like brushing teeth, reading a story, or singing a lullaby.

D. Follow the parents' instructions for bedtime routines, like brushing teeth, reading a story, or singing a lullaby.

34. What does the word disagreements mean in the Dealing with Problems section?

A. Getting long

B. Having fun

C. Arguing

D. Taking a nap

35. What stylistic device does the author use in the conclusion to summarize the main points?

A. Metaphor

B. Quotation

C. Anecdote

D. Repetition

Read the selection and choose the best answer to each question.

A student wrote the following paragraph. Look for corrections that need to be made. Then answer the questions that follow.

(1) Chameleons are weird lizards that change colors and stuff. (2) They live in hot places like desserts and jungles. (3) Chameleons eat bugs with their long, sticky tongues, and they got these funny eyes that go in different ways. (4) They're kinda slow and quite, like, all the time. (5) So, yeah, chameleons are just odd lizards that change colors and eat bugs and live in hot places. (6) Super cool!

36. What is the BEST sentence to replace sentence (1)?

(A) One of the most unique lizards is the chameleon. They are able to do amazing things like change colors!

(B) Chameleons are weird. They are lizards. They change colors and can do other things.

(C) Some lizards are chameleons, which change colors and can do other stuff.

(D) Have you heard of a Chameleon? They're so weird. They are a lizard but change colors.

37. Which word in sentence (2) is spelled incorrectly?
They live in hot places like desserts and jungles.

(A) live

(B) desserts

(C) jungles

(D) places

38. Which option below is the BEST choice to replace sentence (5)?

(A) So, yeah, chameleons are just odd lizards that change colors and eat bugs and live in hot places.

(B) In concluding—chameleons are odd, change colors, eat bugs, and can live in hot places.

(C) As you can see, chameleons are odd lizards that can change colors. They eat bugs, live in hot places, and have other unique features.

(D) There you have it. This is what chameleons are and what they do!

39. The correct spelling of quite from line (4) is—

(A) kite

(B) quitely

(C) quiet

(D) qwiet

40. What stylistic device is used in the phrase "change colors and stuff" in Sentence 1?

(A) Hyperbole

(B) Simile

(C) Colloquial language

(D) Metaphor

41. What is the correct way to write sentence (3)?

(A) Chameleons eat bugs with their long and sticky tongues. They also have funny eyes that can move around in different directions.

(B) Chameleons eat bugs with their long and sticky tongues, and they got these funny eyes that go in different ways.

(C) No change is needed.

(D) Chameleons eat bugs. They have long and sticky tongues. They also have weirdo eyes that can move around in different directions.

42. What is the BEST title for this passage?

(A) Weird Lizards

(B) Cute Chameleons

(C) Chameleons are Lizards

(D) The Animal Kingdom

Read the selection and choose the best answer to each question.

A student wrote the story below. Read the paragraph and look for corrections that need to be made. Then answer the questions that follow.

(1) There was a hamsters. (2) It was small and has fur. (3) The hamster living in a cage. (4) It ran on wheel. (5) It squeeked sometimes. (6) The hamster ate little pelets. (7) It liked to napping.

43. Which is the BEST correction for sentence (1)?

(A) A long time ago there was a hamster.

(B) There were a hamster.

(C) Look–Hamster!

(D) There was a hamsters.

44. Which is the BEST correction for sentence (2)?

(A) It's small…with fur.

(B) It had fur. It was small.

(C) It was small and had fur.

(D) It's smally and furry.

45. Which is the BEST correction for sentence (3)?

(A) The hamster lives in cages.

(B) The hamster lived in a cage.

(C) Cage is where the hamster lived.

(D) And then, it lived in a cage.

46. Which is the BEST correction for sentence (4)?

(A) It ran on a wheel.

(B) Always running on that wheel!

(C) It's running on the weel.

(D) It runned on a wheel.

47. Which is the BEST correction for sentence (5)?

(A) It squeaked some time.

(B) It squeaks so much times!

(C) It squeaked sometimes.

(D) It's squeaking so much of the time!

48. Which is the BEST correction for sentence (6)?

(A) The hamster ate little pelets.

(B) The hamster ate little pellets.

(C) Hamsters eat little pelets.

(D) The hamster is eating the little pelets.

49. Which is the BEST correction for sentence (7)?

(A) It liked to naps.

(B) It likes the napping.

(C) It napped.

(D) It liked to nap.

50. Read the passage below. Rewrite the passage using correct spelling, grammar, and punctuation.

Doing chors is like when you have to do stuff you don't wanna do. It's boring and takes time away from playing games. You have to clean things and pick up stuff, and it's no fun at all. Sometimes, you wish you could just leave everything messy and not do any work. But parents say you have to do chores because it's important, even if you'd rather be doing something else like watching TV or playing with your toys. So, you do the chores, even though you do not want it.

_____

_____

_____

_____

_____

_____

_____

_____

_____

_____

_____

_____

_____

_____

Answers Practice Test 3

1. B, Inspirational and admiring
2. Written answer
3. A, Leader
4. C, The mystery of her final flight.
5. B, Earhart set many records during her lifetime.
6. A, She was a true trailblazer, proving that gender should never hold anyone back from pursuing their dreams.
7. B, By listing her records and daring missions
8. B, Flash-forward
9. A, Dreams really can come true.
10. A, By highlighting their shared goal and teamwork
11. D, It is the beginning of the space flight.
12. C, "One night, as Mia gazed out of the spaceship window, she saw a meteor shower lighting up the dark space."
13. A, They remember where they plant their nuts., D, They are very agile.
14. D, We should appreciate the uniqueness of squirrels.
15. B, They communicate with each other.
16. A, An opinion.
17. C, Sleep, D, Sit
18. C, The story is fiction, but the article is giving information.
19. A, The purpose of the story is to entertain, but the purpose of the article is to give information.
20. B, Rhyme
21. D, The meals are very tasty.
22. A, Enjoy
23. C, He greatly appreciates their hard work.
24. B, Aprons protect their clothes from mess.
25. C, A chef listens to what everyone wants.
26. A, Chefs wake up very early to get started cooking.
27. Written answer
28. C, Juan had never entered the pumpkin carving contest before, but this year was different.
29. A, The festival featured pumpkin picking, apple bobbing, and scarecrow-building contests.
30. D, As the contest kicked off, the timer started, and everyone began their creative work.
31. Juan realized his passion for pumpkins led him to victory, making him smile and very proud.
32. B, To introduce the topic and outline what will be covered
33. D, Follow the parents' instructions for bedtime routines, like brushing teeth, reading a story, or singing a lullaby.
34. C, Arguing
35. D, Repetition
36. A, One of the most unique lizards is the chameleon. They are able to do amazing things like change colors!
37. B, desserts
38. C, As you can see, chameleons are odd lizards that can change colors. They eat bugs, live in hot places, and have other unique features.
39. C, quiet
40. C, Colloquial language
41. A, Chameleons eat bugs with their long and sticky tongues. They also have funny eyes that can move around in different directions.
42. B, Cute Chameleons
43. A, A long time ago there was a hamster.
44. C, It was small and had fur.
45. B, The hamster lived in a cage.
46. A, It ran on a wheel.
47. C, It squeaked sometimes.
48. B, The hamster ate little pellets.
49. B, It liked to nap.
50. Doing chores is when you have to do things you don't want to do. It's boring and takes time away from playing games. You have to clean and pick up things, and it's no fun at all. Sometimes, you wish you could just leave everything messy and not do any work. But parents say you have to do chores because it's important, even if you'd rather be doing something else, like watching TV or playing with your toys. So, you do the chores, even though you do not want to.

PRACTICE TEST 4

GET STARTED →

Read the following passage and answer the questions below.

(1) Once upon a time in the early 1800s, there lived a legendary figure named Davy Crockett. Davy was born in a humble log cabin in the wilderness of Tennessee in 1786. He grew up in the woods, learning to hunt, fish, and become a skilled outdoorsman from a very young age.

(2) Davy Crockett had a strong sense of adventure and bravery. As he got older, he became famous for his incredible skills as a frontiersman. He could track animals for miles and was an expert marksman with his rifle, which he lovingly named "Old Betsy." His remarkable hunting abilities helped feed his family and earned him a reputation as a skilled woodsman.

(3) As a young man, Davy joined the military and fought in the War of 1812. He was known for his courage in battle and quickly became a hero among his fellow soldiers. After the war, he became a politician and served in the United States Congress. But what made him truly famous were his stories about his adventures on the American frontier.

(4) One of his most famous stories was about a wrestling match he had with a bear. He claimed to have wrestled and defeated a bear when he was just a boy. While the tale might have grown taller with time, it showed Davy's bold and fearless spirit.

(5) Davy Crockett's popularity grew even more when he fought in the Battle of the Alamo, a historic battle during the Texas Revolution. Despite the odds, he and his fellow defenders held their ground, and their bravery inspired people all over the world.

(6) Davy Crockett's life ended tragically at the Alamo in 1836, but his legacy as a frontier hero lives on. He is remembered as a symbol of courage, independence, and the American spirit of adventure. His famous motto was, "Be sure you're right, then go ahead," which teaches us to be confident in our beliefs and actions. Davy Crockett's story is a reminder that even a boy from the wilderness can become a legendary figure who inspires generations to come.

1. What narrative technique is used to introduce Davy Crockett in the first paragraph?

(A) Dialogue

(B) Flashback

(C) Chronological introduction

(D) Imagery

2. What is one reason the author presents the information in the article in chronological order? Support your answer with evidence from the article.

_____

_____

_____

_____

_____

_____

_____

_____

3. What is most closely a synonym for the word "reputation" as used in paragraph 2?

(A) Rumor

(B) Job

(C) Politician

(D) Distinction

4. What is the key idea of paragraph 4?

(A) The success of the Battle of the Alamo.

(B) Crockett once wrestled a bear.

(C) Davy's childhood and upbringing.

(D) Crockett was an exceptional hunter and marksman.

5. Based on information found in paragraph 1 and paragraph 2, the reader can conclude that–

(A) The Battle of the Alamo cost many lives.

(B) Crockett proved that you can overcome any adversity that is placed in front of you.

(C) Davy's upbringing made him an expert of the outdoors.

(D) With a lot of practice, Crockett became a very famous soldier.

6. Which sentence is used to support the idea that the story of Crockett wrestling a bear may have been exaggerated?

(A) As a young man, Davy joined the military and fought in the War of 1812.

(B) While the tale might have grown taller with time, it showed Davy's bold and fearless spirit.

(C) Davy Crockett's life ended tragically at the Alamo in 1836, but his legacy as a frontier hero lives on.

(D) Davy Crockett had a strong sense of adventure and bravery.

7. What is the tone of the passage?

(A) Critical and analytical

(B) Nostalgic and melancholic

(C) Admiring and heroic

(D) Humorous and light-hearted

Read the next two selections. Then choose the best answer to each question.

The Championship

(1) Once upon a sunny summer afternoon, in a small town filled with excitement, Andrew was about to experience an unforgettable adventure – playing baseball in the big championship game. With his baseball glove in hand and a cap shading his eyes, he arrived at the baseball field, eager to take part in this thrilling game.

(2) The baseball field was a magical place, with the greenest grass, a bright blue sky overhead, and the sounds of cheers and laughter filling the air. Max's team, the Tigers, was ready to face off against their rivals, the Lions, in a game that would decide the championship.

(3) Max played shortstop, a position that required quick reflexes and a strong arm. His teammates, Sarah, Jake, and Lily, were like family to him, and they had practiced tirelessly for this moment. They had a series of exciting plays, from sliding into bases to making incredible catches in the outfield.

(4) As the game progressed, Max's heart raced with excitement. The score was tied, and it all came down to the last inning. Max was up to bat, and with the bases loaded, he knew he had to give it his all. The pitcher wound up and sent a fastball his way. Max swung with all his might, and the ball soared high into the sky.

(5) The crowd held its breath as the ball sailed over the outfielders' heads and landed just beyond the fence. It was a grand slam home run! Max rounded the bases, cheered on by his teammates and fans, and scored the winning runs.

(6) The Tigers had won the championship, and they celebrated with high-fives, hugs, and a trophy that sparkled in the sunlight. Max felt a mix of joy and pride as he realized that all their hard work and teamwork had paid off.

(7) As the sun set on that magical day, Max knew that this baseball adventure would be a cherished memory for years to come. It taught him about the importance of practice, perseverance, and the thrill of playing as a team. Max couldn't wait for the next baseball season, where new adventures and challenges awaited him on the diamond.

Flourishing Flowers

(1) Flowers are like nature's colorful gems that bring beauty and joy to our world. These amazing plants come in all sorts of shapes, sizes, and colors, and they can be found in gardens, meadows, and even growing by the side of the road. What's truly fascinating is that flowers have a special job in nature – they help plants make new seeds.

(2) Each flower is like a tiny factory, working hard to produce seeds. They use bright colors, sweet scents, and tasty nectar to attract pollinators like bees and butterflies. When these insects visit a flower, they pick up pollen from one flower and carry it to another, which helps the plant create new seeds. This process is essential for growing fruits, vegetables, and many of the plants we rely on for food.

(3) But flowers aren't just practical; they also bring happiness to our lives. Many people love to give and receive bouquets of fresh flowers as gifts for special occasions or just to brighten someone's day. Some flowers even have special meanings, like red roses, which are a symbol of love, and daisies, which represent innocence.

(4) So, the next time you see a beautiful flower, take a moment to appreciate its role in nature's grand plan and the joy it brings to our lives. Flowers remind us that even the smallest things in the natural world can have a big impact on our hearts and our planet.

8. The word "eager" used in paragraph 1 in "The Championship" tells us what about Max?

(A) He is excited about playing in the game.

(B) He is running late to the championship.

(C) He forgot to go to practice the day before.

(D) He is the pitcher for the game today.

9. What technique does the author use to build suspense in paragraph 4?

(A) Detailed description of Max's feelings and actions

(B) Flashback to earlier games

(C) Dialogue between Max and his teammates

(D) Comparison to other sports

10. Read paragraph 7 again from "The Championship". Which sentence below would NOT fit well into this paragraph?

(7) *As the sun set on that magical day, Max knew that this baseball adventure would be a cherished memory for years to come. It taught him about the importance of practice, perseverance, and the thrill of playing as a team. Max couldn't wait for the next baseball season, where new adventures and challenges awaited him on the diamond.*

(A) Max was so proud of his team.

(B) Max appreciated the lessons that his coach taught him and his friends.

(C) Max was up to bat with 3 men on base.

(D) Max was excited for the next season to begin.

11. How is paragraph 4 important to the plot of the story "The Championship"?

- (A) It introduces a new character to the story.
- (B) It is the climax to the story.
- (C) It summarizes the lessons that Max learned.
- (D) It explains the setting of the story.

12. Which literary device is used in the phrase "the baseball field was a magical place"?

- (A) Simile
- (B) Metaphor
- (C) Personification
- (D) Hyperbole

13. What are TWO things flowers do to attract pollinators, according to "Flourishing Flowers"?

- (A) They sing pretty songs.
- (B) They have sweet scents.
- (C) They have bright colors.
- (D) They do fancy dances.

14. What is the central idea of the article "Flourishing Flowers"?

- (A) Even though flowers might be small, they play a big part in our world.
- (B) Flowers come in all different colors.
- (C) Pollinators are important to the ecosystem.
- (D) Bees are an endangered species.

15. Read paragraph 3 again from "Flourishing Flowers". What is the author trying to explain?

(3) But flowers aren't just practical; they also bring happiness to our lives. Many people love to give and receive bouquets of fresh flowers as gifts for special occasions or just to brighten someone's day. Some flowers even have special meanings, like red roses, which are a symbol of love, and daisies, which represent innocence.

(A) Flowers are vital to nature.

(B) Flowers can have different colors, scents, and nectars.

(C) We should appreciate the beauty that flowers can add to our national parks.

(D) Flowers can also be symbols of emotions.

16. Which sentence helps us understand how pollination occurs in the article "Flourishing Flowers"?

(A) When these insects visit a flower, they pick up pollen from one flower and carry it to another, which helps the plant create new seeds.

(B) Many people love to give and receive bouquets of fresh flowers as gifts for special occasions or just to brighten someone's day.

(C) Some flowers even have special meanings, like red roses, which are a symbol of love, and daisies, which represent innocence.

(D) So, the next time you see a beautiful flower, take a moment to appreciate its role in nature's grand plan and the joy it brings to our lives.

17. What literary device is used in the phrase "Flowers are like nature's colorful gems"?

(A) Metaphor

(B) Simile

(C) Personification

(D) Hyperbole

18. Which sentence best illustrates the use of imagery?

(A) "These amazing plants come in all sorts of shapes, sizes, and colors, and they can be found in gardens, meadows, and even growing by the side of the road."

(B) "Each flower is like a tiny factory, working hard to produce seeds."

(C) "When these insects visit a flower, they pick up pollen from one flower and carry it to another, which helps the plant create new seeds."

(D) "Some flowers even have special meanings, like red roses, which are a symbol of love, and daisies, which represent innocence."

19. How does the author emphasize the importance of flowers in nature?

(A) By listing different types of flowers

(B) By explaining how to grow flowers in a garden

(C) By mentioning famous flower gardens around the world

(D) By describing their role in the pollination process

Read the selection and choose the best answer to each question.

(1) In a city filled with hustle and bright streetlight,
A police officer stands, their heart so upright,
With bravery, compassion, and a badge by their side,
They protect and serve with unwavering pride.

(5) With uniform on, and duty in a row,
They keep us safe wherever we go,
They uphold the law, with fairness they pursue,
Justice for all, in all that they do.

(9) In the morning's early light, they're on their beat,
Patrolling our neighborhoods, safeguarding each street,
With courage in their hearts and watchful eyes so keen,
They ensure our city remains serene.

(13) They listen to our worries, big and small,
And answer our calls, giving their all,
With empathy in their hearts and wisdom to share,
They show us that they genuinely care.

(17) When challenges arise and dangers appear,
They say, "We'll protect you; have no fear,"
They build our trust, help our communities believe,
That together we thrive and together we achieve.

(21) With every shift, they strengthen the peace,
Of unity and safety, the goals they release,
To keep our city secure, to aim for the sky,
In their service, we learn to reach high.

(25) So, to the officers who answer the call,
We honor your service, standing tall,
With courage and kindness, you lead the way,
You protect our future, every single day.

20. Which literary device is used in the phrase "With bravery, compassion, and a badge by their side"?

- (A) Simile
- (B) Hyperbole
- (C) Personification
- (D) Alliteration

21. The poet describes police officers as having "unwavering pride" in line 4 in order to show that–

- (A) Police officers are happy to protect their towns.
- (B) Many police officers find the job too difficult.
- (C) Going to school to become a police officer is very expensive.
- (D) Police officers patrol neighborhoods and cities.

22. What does the word keen mean in line 11?

(A) Clean

(B) Disinterested

(C) Bored

(D) Sharp

23. Based on the tone of the poem, how does the author feel about police officers?

(A) They are very tall and strong.

(B) All of them drive either a car or a motorcycle.

(C) It's too dangerous of a job for people to consider.

(D) We must appreciate them for their courage and protection.

24. What is the most likely reason for police officers to have to "strengthen the peace"?

(A) Sometimes neighborhoods can get very loud with music.

(B) Police officers need to work out in the gym to get stronger.

(C) There are bad people in cities and towns who break the law.

(D) It's important to patrol the local businesses and neighborhoods.

25. What stylistic feature is consistently used to create rhythm in the poem?

(A) Free verse

(B) Rhyme

(C) Onomatopoeia

(D) Prose

92

26. How does the author emphasize the dedication of police officers in the poem?

(A) By listing their daily tasks and responsibilities

(B) By comparing them to other professionals

(C) By detailing their personal lives

(D) By highlighting their bravery and compassion

27. Read the poem again. Based on the details in the poem, write a response to the following:

Explain how the police officer feels protecting their city.

Write a well-organized essay from the perspective of the police officer. Use evidence from the poem to support the police officer's perspective.

Remember to:
- Clearly state your central idea
- Organize your writing
- Develop your ideas in detail
- Use evidence from the selection in your response
- Use correct spelling, capitalization, punctuation, and grammar.

Manage your time carefully so that you can:
- Review the selection
- Plan your response
- Write your response
- Revise and edit your response

Read the selection and choose the best answer to each question. As you read the story, look for revisions that need to be made. Answer the questions that follow.

It was happening in Snacksville. Once there lived a boy named Robert who had a deep love for two things: cooking delicious hot dogs and, unsurprisingly, devouring them. Robert was renowned throughout the city for his extraordinary hot dog creations, which he crafted with creativity and care in his family's cozy hot dog stand. But there was one event in Snacksville that made his heart race with excitement every summer – the Great Snacksville Hot Dog Eating Contest.
The contest was the grand finale of Snacksville's annual Food Fiesta, a celebration of all things tasty and delightful. The Fiesta featured cooking competitions food-eating contests and food-themed games. It was a day filled with laughter, music, and, of course, mouthwatering hot dogs of all varieties.
Robert had never entered the hot dog eating contest before, but this year was different. He felt an irresistible urge to prove his love for hot dogs and make a legendary mark on Snacksville's history. With his apron on and a determined gleam in his eye, Robert decided to sign up.
The day of the contest arrived, and the town square buzzed with excitement. There were hot dogs of every flavor and size lined up on tables, ready to be devoured. Robert's eyes were drawn to the grand stage where the hot dog eating contest would take place. There, in the center of it all, was a long table piled high with hot dogs, each one more tantalizing than the last.
Robert joined the other contestants, a mix of kids and adults, each with their own eating strategy. Some had trained for weeks, practicing their hot dog-eating skills, while others simply had an insatiable appetite. Robert, however, relied on his love for hot dogs and a secret weapon – his signature "Snacksville Special" hot dog, loaded with all the tastiest toppings.
As the contest commenced and the timer started, and then everyone dug in. Hot dogs disappeared into mouths, ketchup and mustard flew through the air, and the crowd roared with every bite. Robert, however, savored each mouthful of his own creation, finding joy in every savory and juicy bite.
Minutes passed, and the group of contestants gradually grew smaller. Robert found himself still going strong, feeling full but resolute. He knew he couldn't let Snacksville down. With the last "Snacksville Special" hot dog in front of him, he took a deep breath and devoured it with all his might.
The crowd watched in astonishment as Robert polished off that last hot dog, finishing the entire pile in record time. Cheers erupted, and the judges declared him the winner of the Great Snacksville Hot Dog Eating Contest! Robert had not only triumphed in the contest but had also captured the hearts of his city.
Robert realized that his love for hot dogs had led to his victory as he sat with a belly full of hot dogs and lots of pride in his heart. He celebrated with his friends and family, knowing that this delicious triumph would be a cherished memory in Snacksville for years to come. From that day onward, Robert became known as the "Hot Dog King" of Snacksville, and his love for hot dogs continued to bring joy to the city he adored.

28. Read the first paragraph again. What sentence would be the BEST introduction for this story?

(A) In the beautiful city of Snacksville, there lived a boy named Robert who had a deep love for two things…

(B) Snacksville is where our story takes place. It's about a boy named Robert who had a deep love for two things…

(C) Robert lived in Snacksville. He loved cooking and eating hot dogs both.

(D) There was once a hot dog contest in Snacksville. That's where Robert, a boy, lived.

29. Which sentence below is the corrected version of this sentence from the story:
The Fiesta featured cooking competitions food-eating contests and food-themed games.

(A) The Fiesta featured cooking competitions food-eating contests and food-themed games.

(B) The Fiesta featured cooking competitions. Food-eating contests. Food-themed games.

(C) The Fiesta featured the following: 1. cooking competitions 2. food-eating contests and 3. food-themed games.

(D) The Fiesta featured cooking competitions, food-eating contests, and food-themed games.

30. What is the BEST way to revise this sentence?

As the contest commenced and the timer started, and then everyone dug in.

(A) As the contest commenced the timer started. That's when everyone dug in!

(B) As the contest commenced, the timer started, and everyone dug in.

(C) The contest commenced. The timer started. Everyone dug in.

(D) When the contest commenced the timer started. And everyone dug in?

96

31. This sentence needs to be revised. On the lines provided, rewrite the sentence in a clear and effective way.

Robert realized that his love for hot dogs had led to his victory as he sat with a belly full of hot dogs and lots of pride in his heart.

_____

_____

_____

_____

_____

_____

_____

Read the selection and choose the best answer to each question.
Jackie wrote this paper about owning a pet. Read Jackie's paper and look for revisions she needs to make. Then answer the questions that follow.

How to Be a Super Pet Owner

Introduction: Taking care of a pet is a big responsibility, but it's also super fun! In this paper, we'll learn about the things we can do to be amazing pet owners and keep our furry, feathery, or scaly friends happy and healthy.
Choose the Right Pet: The first step in being a great pet owner is choosing the right pet. You should pick a pet that matches your family's lifestyle and the space you have. Some pets, like dogs and cats, need lots of attention. Maybe others, like fish or hamsters, are more independent.
Feeding Your Pet: Just like you need yummy food to grow big and strong, your pet does too! Make sure to feed your pet the right kind of food. Ask your parents or a vet for advice. Some pets eat special food, so it's important to know what's best for them.
Give Love and Attention: Pets love spending time with their humans. Play with them, pet them, and talk to them. It's a great way to bond with your pet and make them feel happy and loved. Dogs and cats, especially, need lots of cuddles and playtime.
Keep Your Pet Clean: Keeping your pet clean is important for their health. Give your pet baths when needed, trim their nails, and brush their fur or feathers. Some pets, like birds, need clean cages too.

Exercise and Play: Pets, just like you, need exercise to stay healthy. Dogs love going for walks, and cats enjoy playing with toys. Give your pet plenty of opportunities to move and have fun.

Visit the Vet: Sometimes, pets get sick or need a check-up. Take your pet to the vet regularly to make sure they're healthy. Vets can also give your pet vaccines to keep them safe from illnesses.

Provide a Safe Home: Make sure your pet has a safe and cozy place to live. If you have a dog, give them a comfy bed. If you have a fish, make sure their tank is clean and the water is just right. And if you have a bird, provide a clean cage with toys and perches.

Conclusion: Taking care of a pet is a big responsibility, but it's also a lot of fun. Remember to choose the right pet, feed them well, give them love and attention, and keep them clean and healthy.

32. What would be the BEST transitional phrase between the Keep Your Pet Clean paragraph and the Exercise and Play paragraph?

(A) Not only is cleanliness important, so is physical activity.

(B) Now for the next item to consider.

(C) After cleaning is playing games with them.

(D) An example of another important reminder is

33. What is the MOST effective way to combine these two sentences from the Choose the Right Pet section?

Some pets, like dogs and cats, need lots of attention. Maybe others, like fsh or hamsters, are more independent.

(A) Some pets, like dogs and cats, need lots of attention; however, fish or hamsters, are more independent.

(B) Some pets, like dogs and cats, need lots of attention, examples are like fish or hamsters, are more independent.

(C) Some pets, like dogs and cats, need lots of attention. Maybe others, like fish or hamsters, are more independent.

(D) Some pets, like dogs and cats, need lots of attention, while others, like fish or hamsters, are more independent.

34. What does the word opportunities mean in the Exercise and Play section?

(A) Naps

(B) Chances

(C) Snacks

(D) Talks

35. How does the author organize the information in the text?

(A) By telling a story

(B) By listing steps in a process

(C) By comparing different pets

(D) By discussing pros and cons

Read the selection and choose the best answer to each question.
A student wrote the following paragraph. Look for corrections that need to be made. Then answer the questions that follow.

(1) Lemurs are cool creatures found on somewhere called Madagascar. (2) They're not cats, but they're kinda like monkeys, sort of. (3) Lemurs are small and furry with big eyes, and they have long tails that help them balanse on trees. (4) They like to eat fruits, leaves, and bugs, which is their favorite snack. (5) Lemurs live in groups called troops, and they like to jump and play with each other. (6) Some lemurs can even sing and make cool noizes in the jungle. (7) So, lemurs are like these awesome, bouncy animals in Madagascar with big eyes and long tails, and they eat fruits and bugs and sing sometimes. (8) Wow!

36. What is the BEST sentence to replace sentence (1)?

(A) Lemurs are cool creatures found on somewhere called Madagascar.

(B) Lemurs are cool creatures found on Madagascar?

(C) Lemurs are cool creatures found on a faraway island called Madagascar.

(D) Lemurs can be found on Madagascar.

37. Which word in sentence (3) is spelled incorrectly?

Lemurs are small and furry with big eyes, and they have long tails that help them balanse on trees.

(A) balanse

(B) eyes

(C) tails

(D) furry

38. Which option below is the BEST choice to replace sentence (7)?

(A) Lemurs cannot be had as pets, though.

(B) As you can see, lemurs are awesome, bouncy animals in Madagascar. They have unique features like big eyes and long tails.

(C) So, you see, lemurs are like awesome, bouncy, wide eyed, with long tails.

(D) In conclusion, lemurs have loads of fun things, such as big eyes along with long tails. They are awesome!

39. The correct spelling of noizes from line (6) is–

(A) noises

(B) noizes

(C) noices

(D) noyses

100

40. What is the tone of the paragraph?

  (A) Formal and serious

  (B) Critical and analytical

  (C) Informal and enthusiastic

  (D) Melancholic and reflective

41. What is the correct way to write sentence (2)?

  (A) No change is needed

  (B) No, they are not cats. More like monkeys maybe.

  (C) Lemurs are similar to monkeys.

  (D) They aren't cats. They aren't dogs. More like monkeys.

42. What is the BEST title for this passage?

  (A) Lively Lemurs

  (B) The Animal of the Lemur

  (C) What Animals Do You Like?

  (D) Why to Own a Lemur!

Read the selection and choose the best answer to each question.
A student wrote the story below. Read the paragraph and look for corrections that need to be made. Then answer the questions that follow.

(1) There was a fish. (2) It was colorful and swimming in water. (3) The fish lived in a tanc. (4) It's swam around in circles. (5) It blew bubbles some times. (6) The fish ate tiney fish food flakes. (7) It's liked to hide in the plants.

43. Which sentence best illustrates the use of repetition?

(A) Sentence 1

(B) Sentence 2

(C) Sentence 4

(D) Sentence 6

44. Which is the BEST correction for sentence (2)?

(A) It was colorful and liked to swim in the water.

(B) It's colorful. Swims a lot in water.

(C) It's swimming in water and it was colorful.

(D) It was colorful and swimmed in water.

45. Which is the BEST correction for sentence (3)?

(A) The fish lived in a tanc.

(B) The fish lived in a tank.

(C) The fish—upon living in the tank.

(D) It's living—but it's in a tank.

46. Which is the BEST correction for sentence (4)?

(A) It's swam around in circles.

(B) He just goes and goes around in circles.

(C) He swims in cirkles.

(D) It swam around in circles.

47. Which is the BEST correction for sentence (5)?

(A) Sometimes, it blew bubbles.

(B) It's blowing bubbles some times.

(C) There are times when he blew bubble.

(D) At times, blowing bubbles is what it would do.

48. Which is the BEST correction for sentence (6)?

(A) The fish ate tiney fishfood flakes.

(B) The fish eated tiny fish food flakes.

(C) The fish ate tiny fish food flakes.

(D) The food was so tiny, but he ate it–it was fish food.

49. Which is the BEST correction for sentence (7)?

(A) It is really liking to hide in the plants.

(B) It really liked to hide in the plants.

(C) It's hidden in plants allways!

(D) Where is it? Hide in the plants!

50. **Read the passage below. Rewrite the passage using correct spelling, grammar, and punctuation.**

Eating vegitabls is like when you have to eat food that's not very tasty. They're all green and stuff, and you have to chew them, which takes forever. Sometimes, they dont taste good at all, and they're not as yummy as cookies or pizza. You have to eat them because they're healthy, but it's not fun. You might wish you could eat candy all the time insted. But grown-ups say veggies are good for you, so you eat them, even if they're kind of gross.

Answers Practice Test 4

1. C, Chronological introduction
2. Written answer
3. D, Distinction
4. B, Crockett once wrestled a bear.
5. C, Davy's upbringing made him an expert of the outdoors.
6. B, While the tale might have grown taller with time, it showed Davy's bold and fearless spirit.
7. C, Admiring and heroic
8. A, Detailed description of Max's feelings and actions
9. B, Practice and teamwork are important.
10. C, Max was up to bat with 3 men on base.
11. B, It is the climax to the story.
12. B, Metaphor
13. B, They have sweet scents.,C, They have bright colors.
14. A, Even though flowers might be small, they play a big part in our world.
15. D, Flowers can also be symbols of emotions.
16. A, When these insects visit a flower, they pick up pollen from one flower and carry it to another, which helps the plant create new seeds.
17. B, Simile
18. A, "These amazing plants come in all sorts of shapes, sizes, and colors, and they can be found in gardens, meadows, and even growing by the side of the road."
19. D, By describing their role in the pollination process
20. D, Alliteration
21. A, Police officers are happy to protect their towns.
22. D, Sharp
23. D, We must appreciate them for their courage and protection.
24. C, There are bad people in cities and towns who break the law.
25. B, Rhyme
26. D, By highlighting their bravery and compassion
27. Written answer
28. A, In the beautiful city of Snacksville, there lived a boy named Robert who had a deep love for two things…
29. D, The Fiesta featured cooking competitions, food-eating contests, and food-themed games.
30. B, As the contest commenced, the timer started, and everyone dug in.
31. Sitting with a full belly of hot dogs, Robert realized that his affection for these treats had contributed to his victory, filling his heart with pride.
32. A, Not only is cleanliness important, so is physical activity.
33. D, Some pets, like dogs and cats, need lots of attention, while others, like fish or hamsters, are more independent.
34. B, Chances
35. B, By listing steps in a process
36. C, Lemurs are cool creatures found on a faraway island called Madagascar.
37. A, balanse
38. B, As you can see, lemurs are awesome, bouncy animals in Madagascar. They have unique features like big eyes and long tails.
39. A, noises
40. C, Informal and enthusiastic
41. C, Lemurs are similar to monkeys.
42. A, Lively Lemurs
43. C, Sentence 4 ("It's swam around in circles.")
44. A, It was colorful and liked to swim in the water.
45. B, The fish lived in a tank.
46. D, It swam around in circles.
47. A, Sometimes, it blew bubbles.
48. C, The fish ate tiny fish food flakes.
49. B, It really liked to hide in the plants.
50. Eating vegetables is like when you have to consume food that's not very tasty. They're all green and such, and you have to chew them, which can take a while. Sometimes, they don't taste good at all, and they're not as delicious as cookies or pizza. You have to eat them because they're healthy, but it's not particularly enjoyable. You might wish you could eat candy all the time instead. But adults say veggies are good for you, so you eat them, even if they're not your favorite.

PRACTICE TEST 5

GET STARTED →

Read the following passage and answer the questions below.

(1) Long ago, in the 18th century, there lived a remarkable man named George Washington. He was born in 1732 in Virginia and grew up to become one of the most important figures in American history. George was known as the "Father of Our Country" because of the incredible role he played in the founding of the United States of America.

(2) As a young boy, George didn't have fancy toys or video games like we do today. Instead, he learned important skills like farming and surveying. He was strong, hardworking, and always eager to learn. These qualities helped shape him into the great leader he would become.

(3) When George was older, he became a soldier. He fought in a famous conflict called the French and Indian War and learned valuable lessons about leadership and strategy. Later, when the American colonies decided to break free from British rule and become their own country, George Washington was chosen to lead the Continental Army.

(4) One of the most famous moments in George's life happened during the American Revolution. On a freezing night in 1776, his soldiers were tired and hungry. George led them across the icy Delaware River for a daring surprise attack on the enemy. This courageous act turned the tide of the war and gave hope to the American people.

(5) After the Revolutionary War, George Washington could have become a king or dictator, but he chose a different path. He became the first President of the United States in 1789. His leadership helped shape the new nation, and he set important traditions, like serving only two terms as president, which continue today.

(6) George Washington's face can be found on the one-dollar bill, and he is remembered for many things, including his honesty and integrity. You might have heard the story of him chopping down a cherry tree and saying, "I cannot tell a lie." While that story might be a legend, it reminds us of the importance of honesty and truthfulness.

(7) When George Washington passed away in 1799, the entire nation mourned. He left behind a legacy of courage, leadership, and love for his country. Today, we still honor his memory, and his story teaches us that with hard work and dedication, we can achieve great things and help build a better world for future generations. George Washington will forever be a hero in the story of America's founding.

1. How does the author present George Washington's decision not to become a king or dictator?

- (A) As a casual choice
- (B) As a humorous anecdote
- (C) As a significant and principled decision
- (D) As a controversial move

2. What is one reason the author presents the information in the article in chronological order? Support your answer with evidence from the article.

_____

_____

_____

_____

_____

_____

_____

_____

_____

_____

_____

3. What is most closely a synonym for the word "dedication" as used in paragraph 7?

(A) Annoyance

(B) Paradox

(C) Definition

(D) Commitment

4. What is the key idea of paragraph 4?

(A) Washington was a brave leader during the Revolutionary War.

(B) Washington was known as the "Father of our Country".

(C) The $1 bill has his face on it.

(D) The country was sad when he passed away.

5. Which sentence best illustrates the use of imagery?

(A) "He was born in 1732 in Virginia."

(B) "He learned important skills like farming and surveying."

(C) "On a freezing night in 1776, his soldiers were tired and hungry."

(D) "George Washington's face can be found on the one-dollar bill."

6. Which sentence is used to support the idea that Washington's childhood helped to make him the man he became later in life?

(A) These qualities helped shape him into the great leader he would become.

(B) As a young boy, George didn't have fancy toys or video games like we do today.

(C) George Washington will forever be a hero in the story of America's founding.

(D) While that story might be a legend, it reminds us of the importance of honesty and truthfulness.

109

7. What is the main purpose of the final paragraph?

(A) To summarize George Washington's military achievements

(B) To highlight the personal anecdotes about George Washington

(C) To emphasize George Washington's enduring legacy and influence

(D) To describe the mourning period after his death

Read the next two selections. Then choose the best answer to each question.

A New Sister

(1) Once upon a time, in a cozy home filled with love, there was a fifth-grader named Emily who was about to embark on a beautiful adventure – welcoming a new baby sister into her family. With her heart brimming with excitement and curiosity, she prepared for the day her family would grow.

(2) The day finally arrived when Emily's parents brought her to the hospital to meet her new baby sister. As she peered into the tiny crib, her heart melted at the sight of the precious bundle wrapped in a soft pink blanket. She gently touched the baby's tiny fingers, feeling the warmth of a new life.

(3) Emily's baby sister, whom they named Lily, quickly became the apple of everyone's eye. Emily took on her new role as a big sister with pride, helping her parents change diapers, sing lullabies, and even telling Lily stories from her favorite books.

(4) As the days turned into weeks, Emily noticed how her family's love expanded to include this tiny newcomer. She learned about the joys and challenges of having a baby in the house. Late nights turned into tender moments as she rocked Lily to sleep, humming sweet melodies.

(5) One day, Emily's parents asked her to choose a special gift for Lily. Emily picked out a soft, cuddly teddy bear, hoping it would become her baby sister's first best friend. Seeing Lily's eyes light up when she received the gift made Emily's heart swell with happiness.

(6) As Lily grew, Emily watched her baby sister take her first steps, say her first words, and explore the world with wide-eyed wonder. She realized that being a big sister meant not only sharing toys and stories but also being a role model and a source of comfort and support.

(7) Emily's love for her sister continued to grow with each passing day. She knew that the adventure of having a new baby sister had changed her life in beautiful ways. Emily couldn't wait to see all the wonderful adventures and milestones that awaited her and Lily as they navigated the journey of sisterhood together, hand in hand.

Dazzling Dolphins

(1) Dolphins are incredible and intelligent creatures that live in the world's oceans. These amazing animals are known for their friendly nature and playful behavior. Dolphins come in various shapes and sizes, but they all share some common features like a sleek, smooth body, a dorsal fin on their backs, and a long snout filled with sharp teeth.

(2) One of the coolest things about dolphins is that they are excellent swimmers. They can leap out of the water and perform acrobatic tricks, which is always a joy to watch. Dolphins are also known for their communication skills. They use a series of clicks and whistles to talk to each other and even have unique "signature whistles" that act like names. This helps them stay connected in the big, wide ocean.

(3) What's even more fascinating is that dolphins are known for their kindness. They often help other animals, including humans, who are in trouble at sea. Some stories even tell of dolphins guiding lost sailors back to shore. So, the next time you see these marvelous creatures in a book or at an aquarium, remember that dolphins are not only smart and playful but also incredibly kind-hearted beings of the sea.

8. What stylistic device is used to create imagery in the passage?

- (A) Metaphors
- (B) Symbolism
- (C) Vivid descriptions
- (D) Irony

9. What is the main theme of the passage?

- (A) The importance of education
- (B) The value of hard work
- (C) The joy and responsibility of sibling relationships
- (D) The challenges of moving to a new home

10. Which sentence best illustrates the use of personification?

- (A) "Her heart brimming with excitement and curiosity."
- (B) "Emily's baby sister, whom they named Lily, quickly became the apple of everyone's eye."
- (C) "Emily picked out a soft, cuddly teddy bear."
- (D) "Emily's love for her sister continued to grow with each passing day."

11. How is paragraph 4 important to the plot of the story "A New Sister"?

(A) It describes the setting of the house where Emily lives.

(B) It gives a history of when Emily first learned she would become a big sister.

(C) It begins to show us the adjustments to having a new sister.

(D) It introduces new characters into the story.

12. Which paragraph primarily focuses on Emily's role as a big sister?

(A) Paragraph 2

(B) Paragraph 3

(C) Paragraph 4

(D) Paragraph 5

13. What are TWO things all dolphins have in common, according to "Dazzling Dolphins"?

(A) Dorsal fins.

(B) They enjoy doing tricks.

(C) Body shape.

(D) A long snout.

14. What is the central idea of the article "Dazzling Dolphins"?

(A) Dolphins come in many shapes and sizes.

(B) Dolphins are an endangered animal.

(C) We can feed dolphins all kinds of fish and sea life.

(D) We should appreciate the uniqueness and kindness of dolphins.

15. Read paragraph 3 again from "Dazzling Dolphins". What is a reason that the author gives us to appreciate dolphins?

(3) What's even more fascinating is that dolphins are known for their kindness. They often help other animals, including humans, who are in trouble at sea. Some stories even tell of dolphins guiding lost sailors back to shore. So, the next time you see these marvelous creatures in a book or at an aquarium, remember that dolphins are not only smart and playful but also incredibly kind-hearted beings of the sea.

(A) They are kind and helpful animals.

(B) They help eat fish that are overpopulated.

(C) They are beautiful and graceful creatures.

(D) They can communicate underwater for many miles.

16. Which sentence uses compare and contrast in "Dazzling Dolphins"?

(A) Dolphins are incredible and intelligent creatures that live in the world's oceans.

(B) These amazing animals are known for their friendly nature and playful behavior.

(C) Dolphins come in various shapes and sizes, but they all share some common features like a sleek, smooth body, a dorsal fin on their backs, and a long snout filled with sharp teeth.

(D) One of the coolest things about dolphins is that they are excellent swimmers.

17. What TWO words are antonyms for the word "various" used in paragraph 1 of "Dazzling Dolphins"?

(A) Many

(B) Few

(C) One

(D) Several

18. How does the author emphasize the intelligence of dolphins?

(A) By describing their physical features

(B) By detailing their communication skills and social behavior

(C) By comparing them to other sea creatures

(D) By highlighting their diet and hunting methods

19. What narrative perspective is used in the passage?

(A) First person

(B) Second person

(C) Third person limited

(D) Third person omniscient

Read the selection and choose the best answer to each question.

(1) On a battlefield filled with courage so bright,
A soldier stands tall, their heart filled with might,
With bravery, honor, and a uniform so wide,
They defend our land with unwavering pride.

(5) With armor and rifle, they march in a row,
Facing challenges that only heroes know,
They protect our nation, in battles they pursue,
Preserving our freedom, so skies remain blue.

(9) In the morning's early light, they're on the line,
Guarding our borders, come rain or sunshine,
With steadfast hearts and eyes sharp and keen,
They ensure our homeland remains serene.

(13) They listen to orders, big and small,
And face adversity, giving their all,
With dedication in their hearts and wisdom to share,
They show us that they genuinely care.

(17) When dangers arise and enemies near,
They say, "We'll stand strong; have no fear,"
They build our trust, help our nation believe,
That together we triumph and together we achieve.

(21) With every mission, they protect the peace,
Of liberty and justice, their goals never cease,
To safeguard our land, to aim for the sky,
In their service, we learn to reach high.

(25) To the soldiers standing strong and brave,
We honor your courage, the sacrifices you gave,
You're the guardians of our freedom, it's clear and true,
Our nation stands taller because of you.

20. What is the main theme of the poem?

(A) The everyday life of a soldier

(B) The importance of military strategy

(C) The bravery and dedication of soldiers in protecting their nation

(D) The historical events involving soldiers

21. The poet describes the soldiers as having "unwavering pride" in line 4 in order to show that–

(A) The flag will continue to fly high.

(B) The soldiers are very tall and can see over obstacles.

(C) They love their country.

(D) Soldiers do not want to protect their country.

116

22. What does the word cease mean in line 22?

- (A) End
- (B) Continue
- (C) Flourish
- (D) Beautiful

23. Based on the tone of the poem, how does the author feel about soldiers?

- (A) They are weak and afraid.
- (B) They are too young to go to war.
- (C) We should all sign up to become soldiers.
- (D) We must appreciate them for their courage and protection.

24. What is the most likely reason for soldiers to have to "protect the peace"?

- (A) Because some people in other countries are very loud.
- (B) Our country has enemies that want to harm us.
- (C) They are paid large sums of money to do this job.
- (D) They went to school to know how to handle the weapons.

25. Which sentence best illustrates the use of personification?

- (A) "With armor and rifle, they march in a row,"
- (B) "With steadfast hearts and eyes sharp and keen,"
- (C) "They listen to orders, big and small,"
- (D) "Our nation stands taller because of you."

26. Notice the imagery used in line 10 from the poem. *"come rain or sunshine"* This line symbolizes–

(A) The weather differs from day to day.

(B) Soldiers do not need to battle during the winter months because it is so cold.

(C) Battles only occur during certain seasons of the year.

(D) Soldiers will fight to protect us no matter what.

27. Read the poem again. Based on the details in the poem, write a response to the following:

Explain how the soldier might be feeling about being in battle.

Write a well-organized essay from the perspective of the soldier. Use evidence from the poem to support the soldier's perspective.

Remember to:
- Clearly state your central idea
- Organize your writing
- Develop your ideas in detail
- Use evidence from the selection in your response
- Use correct spelling, capitalization, punctuation, and grammar.

Manage your time carefully so that you can:
- Review the selection
- Plan your response
- Write your response
- Revise and edit your response

Read the selection and choose the best answer to each question. As you read the story, look for revisions that need to be made. Answer the questions that follow.

There was a town named Berryville. There lived a girl named Julie who had a love for two things: baking and, unsurprisingly, eating. Julie was known far and wide for her delightful pies, which she created with love and care in her cozy kitchen. But there was one event in Berryville that made her heart race with excitement every year – the Great Berryville Pie Eating Contest.

The contest was the highlight of the town's annual Berry Festival, a celebration of all things fruity and delicious. The festival featured pie baking competitions pie-eating contests and pie-themed games. It was a day filled with laughter, music, and, of course, pies of all kinds.

Julie had never entered the pie eating contest before, but this year was different. She felt an urge to prove her love for pies and make her mark on Berryville history. With her apron on and a determined twinkle in her eye, Julie decided to sign up.
The day of the contest arrived, and the town square buzzed with excitement. There were pies of all flavors and sizes lined up on tables, ready to be devoured. Julie's eyes were drawn to the grand stage where the pie eating contest would take place. There, in the middle of it all, was a long table covered in pies, each one more tempting than the last.

Julie joined the other contestants, a mix of kids and adults, each with their own strategy. Some had trained for weeks, practicing their pie-eating skills, while others simply had an insatiable appetite. Julie, however, relied on her love for pies and a secret weapon – her homemade berry pie.
As the contest began and the timer started, and everyone dug in. Pies flew into faces, whipped cream smeared everywhere, and the crowd cheered with every bite. Julie, however, savored each mouthful of her own pie, finding joy in every sweet and tangy bite.

Minutes passed, and the field of contestants dwindled. Julie found herself still going strong, feeling full but determined. She knew she couldn't let Berryville down. With the last slice of her pie in front of her, she took a deep breath and dug in with all her might.
The crowd watched in awe as Julie devoured that last piece, finishing her entire pie in record time. Cheers erupted, and the judges announced her as the winner of the Great Berryville Pie Eating Contest! Julie had not only conquered the contest but also captured the hearts of her town.

Her belly was full of pie and her heart was full of pride and it was then that Julie realized that her love for pies had led her to victory. She celebrated with her friends and family, knowing that this sweet victory would be a cherished memory in Berryville for years to come. From that day forward, Julie became known as the "Pie Queen" of Berryville, and her love for pies continued to bring joy to the town she adored.

28. Read the first paragraph again.

There was a town named Berryville. There lived a girl named Julie who had a love for two things: baking and, unsurprisingly, eating. Julie was known far and wide for her delightful pies, which she created with love and care in her cozy kitchen. But there was one event in Berryville that made her heart race with excitement every year – the Great Berryville Pie Eating Contest.

What sentence would be the BEST introduction for this story?

(A) There was a town named Berryville and a girl named Julie. She loved baking and eating.

(B) Once, in a town named Berryville, there lived a girl named Julie who had a love for two things: baking and, unsurprisingly, eating.

(C) This story is about Julie, Berryville, baking and eating!

(D) Once upon a time, Julie from Berryville loved to eat and bake.

29. Which sentence below is the corrected version of this sentence from the story:

The festival featured pie baking competitions pie-eating contests and pie-themed games.

(A) The festival featuring pie baking competitions pie-eating contests and pie-themed games.

(B) The festival features pie baking competitions, pie-eating contests, and pie-themed games?

(C) The festival featured pie baking competitions, pie-eating contests, and pie-themed games.

(D) The festival. Featured pie baking competitions, pie-eating contests. It also had pie-themed games.

30. What is the BEST way to revise this sentence?

As the contest began and the timer started, and everyone dug in.

(A) As the contest began, the timer started, and everyone dug in.

(B) When the contest started, the timer started, and everyone started too.

(C) As the contest began, the timer started. Everyone dug in too.

(D) The timer started which signaled the start of the contest, so then everyone dug in.

31. This sentence needs to be revised. On the lines provided, rewrite the sentence in a clear and effective way.

Her belly was full of pie and her heart was full of pride and it was then that Julie realized that her love for pies had led her to victory.

_____

_____

_____

_____

_____

_____

Read the selection and choose the best answer to each question.
Tommy wrote this paper about recycling. Read Tommy's paper and look for revisions he needs to make. Then answer the questions that follow.

The Amazing World of Recycling

Introduction: Recycling is super cool, and I'm here to tell you all about it! It's like magic that helps our planet. In this paper, we'll explore what recycling is, why it's important, and some easy ways we can all recycle to make the Earth a better place.

What is Recycling? Recycling is like when you give old stuff a second chance to be something new and awesome.

It's like turning an old superhero costume into a brand new cape! Recycling helps us use less new stuff, which saves trees, energy, and even water.

Why is Recycling Important? Recycling is a big deal because it helps our planet stay healthy. When we recycle, we use less of Earth's resources. That means fewer trees get cut down for paper, less oil gets used for plastic, and less metal is mined for cans. Plus, it reduces the trash we throw away, which is great for our environment.

Recycling Helps Animals: Animals, like cute polar bears and amazing sea turtles, depend on us to take care of the planet. When we recycle, we keep their homes clean and safe. Recycling also means less trash in the ocean, which is super important for sea creatures.

How Can We Recycle? Recycling is easy! We can start by sorting our trash. There are special bins for paper. There are also bins for plastic, glass, and cans. Make sure to put the right stuff in the right bin. Then, those things can be turned into new stuff.

Here are some cool recycling ideas:

- Reuse old cardboard boxes for fun art projects.
- Turn old clothes into colorful rags.
- Use both sides of the paper when drawing or writing.
- Ask your family to buy products made from recycled materials.

Conclusion: Recycling is like a superhero that helps our Earth stay clean and green. By recycling, we save trees, protect animals, and keep our planet happy. So, let's all do our part and recycle to make our world a better place for everyone, including cute animals and future generations!

32. What would be the BEST transitional phrase between the Why is Recycling Important paragraph and the Recycling Helps Animals paragraph?

A) And what about animals?

B) Not only will recycling help the environment, it also helps wildlife.

C) Now that you understand why recycling is important, let's talk about something else.

D) Here's another example of why recycling is important.

33. What is the MOST effective way to combine these two sentences from the How Can We Recycle section?

There are special bins for paper. There are also bins for plastic, glass, and cans.

(A) There are special bins for paper. There are also bins for plastic, glass, and cans.

(B) There are special bins for the following items: paper, plastic, glass, and cans.

(C) There are special bins for lots of things like paper plastic glass and even cans.

(D) There are special bins for paper, plastic, glass, and cans.

34. What does the word sorting mean in the How Can We Recycle section?

(A) Seperating

(B) Combining

(C) Recycling

(D) Throwing

35. Which sentence can BEST be added at the end of the Conclusion section to bring this paper to a more effective ending?

(A) Recycling is good.

(B) Recycling will help our world for years to come!

(C) Don't forget to separate your trash to make recycling easier.

(D) Plastic is the most difficult item to recycle, so make sure to recycle plastic!

Read the selection and choose the best answer to each question.

A student wrote the following paragraph. Look for corrections that need to be made. Then answer the questions that follow.

(1) Lions are big cats with fur and stuff. (2) They live in Africa and sometimes in other places too. (3) Lions are the kings of the jungle and they rore really loud. (4) They eat animals like zebras and antelopes because they're hungary. (5) Lions have manes, which are like fluffy hair, and they use them to look fancy. (6) They have families called prides, and they play and sleep a lot. (7) So, lions are like, big cats that live in Africa and roar and eat stuff. (8) Yeah.

36. What is the BEST sentence to replace sentence (1)?

(A) Lions. They are big cats. They have fur and lots of other stuff.

(B) Lions are big cats with fur and other things.

(C) Lions are big cats with beautiful fur and several other fun features.

(D) Lions! They have fur and are really big cats!

37. Which word in sentence (3) is spelled incorrectly?

Lions are the kings of the jungle and they rore really loud.

(A) lions

(B) kings

(C) jungle

(D) rore

38. Which option below is the BEST choice to replace sentence (7)?

(A) As we have learned, lions are huge cats that live in Africa. They are fantastic and unique animals. No wonder they are called the King of the Jungle!

(B) In conclusion, lions are big cats which roar and eat other animals. Watch out!

(C) Let's go on a safari today!

(D) But don't ever try to have a lion as a pet! They are too dangerous!

39. The correct spelling of hungary from line (4) is–

(A) hungary

(B) hungrey

(C) hungry

(D) Hunger

40. What literary device is used in the phrase "Lions are the kings of the jungle"?

(A) Simile

(B) Hyperbole

(C) Metaphor

(D) Personification

41. What is the correct way to write sentence (2)?

(A) No change is needed

(B) Lions live in many locations, but can primarily be found in Africa.

(C) Do you think lions only live in Africa? Well, you'd be wrong. They live all over.

(D) Lions live in Africa. They also live in other places too.

42. What is the BEST title for this passage?

(A) Cute Cats

(B) Life in Africa

(C) Let's learn!

(D) The King of the Jungle

Read the selection and choose the best answer to each question.

A student wrote the story below. Read the paragraph and look for corrections that need to be made. Then answer the questions that follow.

(1) There was ferret. (2) It was playful and had softly fur. (3) The ferret lived in a cozzy cage. (4) It zoomed around and playing with toys. (5) It made little chittering sounds some times. (6) The ferret nibbled on special ferret foods lots. (7) It liked to curl up in a fluffy blankets.

43. Which sentence contains a missing article that needs correction?

(A) Sentence 1

(B) Sentence 2

(C) Sentence 3

(D) Sentence 4

44. Which is the BEST correction for sentence (2)?

(A) It was playful and had soft fur.

(B) It was playful. It had soft fur.

(C) It was playful and had softly fur.

(D) It's soft fur was playful.

45. Which is the BEST correction for sentence (3)?

(A) The ferret lives in a cozzy cage.

(B) It lived in a cozy cages.

(C) It's living, but only in a cozy cage.

(D) The ferret lived in a cozy cage.

46. What is the main idea of the paragraph?

(A) The ferret's playful nature and its cozy living environment.

(B) The ferret's interaction with other animals.

(C) The ferret's health issues and dietary restrictions.

(D) The ferret's history and origin.

47. Which is the BEST correction for sentence (5)?

(A) It makes little chittering sounds some times.

(B) Listen! It's chittering some times!

(C) It made little chittering sounds sometimes.

(D) Sometimes, it chitters, but not allways.

48. Which is the BEST correction for sentence (6)?

(A) The ferret nibbled on special ferret foods lots.

(B) The ferret nibbled on special ferret food.

(C) Nibbling, the ferret ate lots of food.

(D) The ferret eats by nibbling on lots of food.

49. Which is the BEST correction for sentence (7)?

(A) See, he likes to curl up in fluffy blankets, aw!

(B) It liked to curl up in a fluffy blankets.

(C) It liked to curl up in fluffy blankets.

(D) In fluffy blankets, said ferret curls up.

50. **Read the passage below. Rewrite the passage using correct spelling, grammar, and punctuation.**

Homewrok is like school work you do at home. Its not fun, becuz you have to do it after school when you want to play. You have to sit and do stuff you learned in class and it takes a long time. Sometimes, you dont understand it, and it makes you feel tired and grumpy. You wish you could watch TV or play games instead. But you have to do it, and it's boring and yucky.

_____

_____

_____

_____

_____

_____

_____

_____

_____

_____

_____

_____

_____

_____

_____

Answers Practice Test 5

1. C, As a significant and principled decision
2. Written answer
3. D, Commitment
4. A, Washington was a brave leader during the Revolutionary War.
5. C, "On a freezing night in 1776, his soldiers were tired and hungry."
6. A, These qualities helped shape him into the great leader he would become.
7. C, To emphasize George Washington's enduring legacy and influence
8. C, Vivid descriptions
9. C, The joy and responsibility of sibling relationships
10. A, "Her heart brimming with excitement and curiosity."
11. C, It begins to show us the adjustments to having a new sister.
12. B, Paragraph 3
13. A, Dorsal fins., D, A long snout.
14. D, We should appreciate the uniqueness and kindness of dolphins.
15. A, They are kind and helpful animals.
16. C, Dolphins come in various shapes and sizes, but they all share some common features like a sleek, smooth body, a dorsal fin on their backs, and a long snout filled with sharp teeth.
17. B, Few, C, One
18. B, By detailing their communication skills and social behavior
19. D, Third person omniscient
20. C, The bravery and dedication of soldiers in protecting their nation
21. C, They love their country.
22. A, End
23. D, We must appreciate them for their courage and protection.
24. B, Our country has enemies that want to harm us.
25. D, "Our nation stands taller because of you."
26. D, Soldiers will fight to protect us no matter what.
27. Written answer
28. B, Once, in a town named Berryville, there lived a girl named Julie who had a love for two things: baking and, unsurprisingly, eating.
29. C, The festival featured pie baking competitions, pie-eating contests, and pie-themed games.
30. B, When the contest started, the timer started, and everyone started too.
31. Julie felt really proud with a full belly of pie, realizing that her love for pies helped her win.
32. B, Not only will recycling help the environment, it also helps wildlife.
33. D, There are special bins for paper, plastic, glass, and cans.
34. A, Seperating
35. B, Recycling will help our world for years to come!
36. C, Lions are big cats with beautiful fur and several other fun features.
37. D, rore
38. A, As we have learned, lions are huge cats that live in Africa. They are fantastic and unique animals. No wonder they are called the King of the Jungle!
39. C, hungry
40. C, Metaphor
41. B, Lions live in many locations, but can primarily be found in Africa.
42. D, The King of the Jungle
43. A, Sentence 1 ("There was ferret." should be "There was a ferret.")
44. A, It was playful and had soft fur.
45. D, The ferret lived in a cozy cage.
46. A, The ferret's playful nature and its cozy living environment.
47. C, It made little chittering sounds sometimes.
48. B, The ferret nibbled on special ferret food.
49. C, It liked to curl up in fluffy blankets.
50. Homework is like schoolwork you do at home. It's not fun because you have to do it after school when you want to play. You have to sit and work on things you learned in class, and it takes a long time. Sometimes, you don't understand it, and it can make you feel tired and grumpy. You wish you could watch TV or play games instead. But you have to do it, and it's boring and not enjoyable.

STAAR

STATE OF TEXAS ASSESSMENTS OF ACADEMIC READINESS

GRADE 5
MATHEMATICS

Jason Reed

Second Edition

Table of Contents

Introduction

About the Math STAAR Tests

The 5th-grade Math STAAR test includes a total of 50 questions. Among these, 47 are multiple-choice questions where students must choose the correct answer from the provided options. The remaining 3 questions are open-ended, requiring students to express their thoughts and provide explanations.

About the Math STAAR Practice Tests in This Book

The 5 practice tests included in this book are designed to replicate the Math STAAR tests accurately. They provide your child with a valuable opportunity to understand key concepts and familiarize themselves with the format, types of questions, and time constraints they will encounter on the STAAR test.

Repetition is a proven method for effective studying. We firmly believe in the power of practice, which is why we've included five carefully crafted practice tests in this book.

By working through these practice tests, your child can:

- **Improve time management:** They will become adept at managing their time efficiently during the test, ensuring they complete all sections within the allocated time.
- **Build confidence:** Repeatedly solving questions in a format similar to the actual test will boost their confidence, reducing anxiety on test day.

- **Identify weaknesses:** These tests will help pinpoint specific areas where your child may need additional review and practice.
- **Enhance problem-solving skills:** Regular practice hones problem-solving skills and strategies, enabling your child to tackle challenging questions effectively.
- **Score higher:** Through focused practice and familiarization with the test structure, your child can strive for higher scores on the STAAR test.

The questions in these practice tests closely mirror those found in the actual STAAR tests, ensuring that your child gains a deep understanding of the test's structure and content. By working through these practice tests, they will be well-equipped to achieve success on the Math STAAR test.

As parents, educators, or instructors, your support and encouragement play a pivotal role in your child's academic journey. We encourage you to actively engage with your child's mathematics education, using these resources as tools to enhance their learning experience.

To All Parents and Teachers,

Thank you for purchasing the STAAR Mathematics Practice Workbook for Grade 5.

As an independent author, I have put a great deal of effort into ensuring the quality and accuracy of the content provided. Each problem has been carefully solved and reviewed to provide the best learning experience.

However, despite the rigorous efforts to maintain high standards, occasional mistakes can occur. If you come across any errors or discrepancies in the book or the solutions, please do not hesitate to reach out. Your feedback is invaluable in helping to improve the quality of this workbook.

For any corrections, questions, or comments, please contact me at *jasonreedbooks@gmail.com*. Your assistance in identifying and rectifying any issues is greatly appreciated.

Thank you for your understanding and support.

Sincerely,

Jason Reed

PRACTICE TEST 1

GET STARTED →

1. If a recipe for one loaf of bread requires 0.75 cups of sugar, how many cups of sugar are needed to make 9 loaves of bread?

(A) 5.75 cups of sugar

(B) 6.75 cups of sugar

(C) 7.75 cups of sugar

(D) 8.75 cups of sugar

2. Which numbers have a value greater than 1.0073? Choose two correct answers.

(A) 1.00079

(B) 1.0065

(C) 1.04

(D) 1.00099

(E) 1.0078

3. Sarah's backpack weighs 2.75 ounces. James' backpack is $3\frac{1}{4}$ ounces heavier than Sarah's backpack. What is the weight in kilograms of James' backpack?

(A) 5 ounces

(B) 5.5 ounces

(C) 6 ounces

(D) 6.5 ounces

4. Maria imagined a number. If she multiplies it by 4 and then divides the result by 3, she gets a number that is three times greater than the difference between her original number and 15. What number did Maria imagine?

- (A) 8
- (B) 9
- (C) 10
- (D) 27

5. The graph represents the temperature in Fahrenheit measured at the same time each day of the week. The average temperature for this week is:

- (A) 23.2 °F
- (B) 23.4 °F
- (C) 23.6 °F
- (D) 23.8 °F

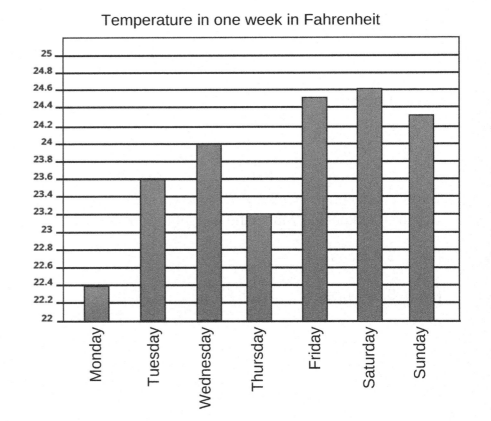

Temperature in one week in Fahrenheit

6. The table represents a relationship between the number of months (*x*) and the amount of savings (y) in dollars.

x	y
3	450
6	900
9	1350
12	1800

Which statement about the relationship between the number of months (x) and amount of savings (y) is true?

A It is a multiplicative pattern because each x-value is determined by multiplying the corresponding y-value by 3.

B It is a multiplicative pattern because each y-value is determined by multiplying the corresponding x-value by 150.

C It is an additive pattern because each y-value can be determined by finding the sum of the previous x- and y-values.

D It is an additive pattern because each y-value is determined by adding 150 to the corresponding x-value.

7. The chessboard has an area of 576 square inches. The area of one chess square is:

A 7,5 square inches

B 8 square inches

C 9 square inches

D 9.5 square inches

8. A chef has 36.5 gallons of soup and wants to serve it equally among 5 bowls. How many gallons of soup will each bowl contain?

- (A) 7.3 gallons
- (B) 8 gallons
- (C) 8.5 gallons
- (D) 9.3 gallons

9. A mechanic divided 75.2 gallons of oil equally into 4 containers. How many gallons of oil were in each container?

- (A) 18.8 gallons
- (B) 20.2 gallons
- (C) 26 gallons
- (D) 28.2 gallons

10. Which cube has a perimeter of 102 inches?

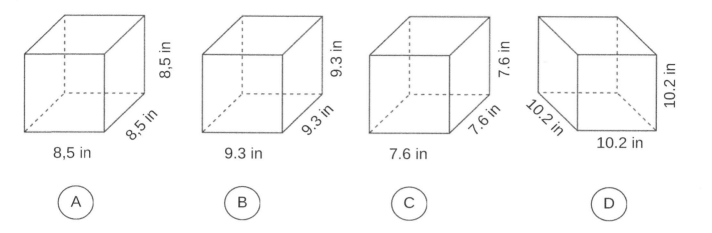

8,5 in   8,5 in   8,5 in

9.3 in   9.3 in   9.3 in

7.6 in   7.6 in   7.6 in

10.2 in   10.2 in   10.2 in

A   B   C   D

11. Four teams competed in a basketball tournament. The bar graph illustrates the number of points scored by each team. What fraction of the total points scored were by Team D?

A $\frac{6}{20}$

B $\frac{6}{29}$

C $\frac{8}{23}$

D $\frac{7}{29}$

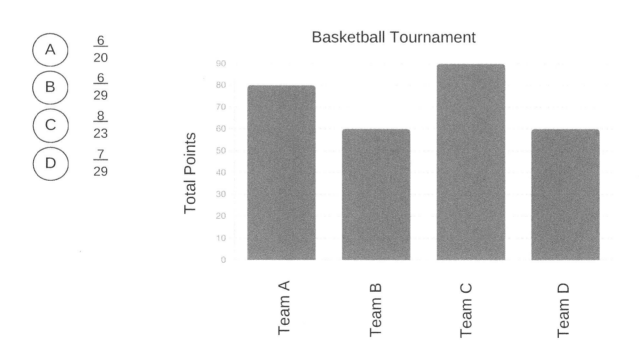

Basketball Tournament

9

12. A box contains 180 candies. There are 25 chocolate candies and 70 lollipops. The rest of the candies are gumdrops. Which equation can be used to find t, the total number of gumdrops in the box?

(A) t = 180-25-70

(B) t = 180-25+70

(C) t = 180+25-70

(D) t = 180+25+70

13. A recipe calls for a total of $\frac{3}{4}$ cups of sweet ingredients. You have already added $\frac{1}{3}$ cups of sugar and $\frac{1}{6}$ cups of honey. The rest of the sweet ingredients will come from maple syrup. Which equation can be used to find m, the amount of maple syrup needed?

(A) $m = \frac{3}{4} - \frac{1}{3} - \frac{1}{6}$

(B) $m = \frac{3}{4} + \frac{1}{6} - \frac{1}{3}$

(C) $m = \frac{1}{6} + \frac{3}{4} - \frac{1}{3}$

(D) $m = \frac{1}{3} + \frac{1}{6} - \frac{3}{4}$

10

14. Find the value of the expression: $(15 \cdot 3 + 7) : 4 =$

   Ⓐ 12

   Ⓑ 13

   Ⓒ 14

   Ⓓ 15

15. Find the value of the expression: $(85 : 5 + 9) - (7 + 8 \cdot 2) =$

   Ⓐ 0

   Ⓑ 1

   Ⓒ 2

   Ⓓ 3

16. Find the value of the expression: $((32 \cdot 3 - 12) \cdot 2 + (75 : 5 + 6) : 3) : 25 =$

   Ⓐ 7

   Ⓑ 10

   Ⓒ 12

   Ⓓ 15

17. Simplify the expression: $\dfrac{3}{4} \cdot \left(\dfrac{2}{3} + \dfrac{1}{6}\right) =$

   Ⓐ $\dfrac{5}{8}$

   Ⓑ $\dfrac{1}{3}$

   Ⓒ $\dfrac{3}{7}$

   Ⓓ $\dfrac{1}{9}$

18. Simplify the expression: $\left(\dfrac{5}{6} - \dfrac{1}{3}\right) : \dfrac{1}{2} =$

(A) $\dfrac{1}{3}$

(B) $\dfrac{1}{6}$

(C) 1

(D) 2

19. Simplify the expression: $\left(\dfrac{2}{3} \cdot \dfrac{1}{6}\right) + \left(\dfrac{2}{3} \cdot \dfrac{1}{6}\right) =$

(A) $\dfrac{1}{2}$

(B) $\dfrac{1}{9}$

(C) $\dfrac{2}{6}$

(D) $\dfrac{2}{9}$

20. Find the value of the unknown fractions marked with the letters a, b, and c on the diagram:

(A) $a = \dfrac{1}{4}$, $b = \dfrac{1}{8}$, $c = \dfrac{1}{16}$

(B) $a = \dfrac{1}{8}$, $b = \dfrac{1}{2}$, $c = \dfrac{1}{24}$

(C) $a = \dfrac{1}{3}$, $b = \dfrac{1}{9}$, $c = \dfrac{1}{10}$

(D) $a = \dfrac{1}{2}$, $b = \dfrac{1}{4}$, $c = \dfrac{1}{12}$

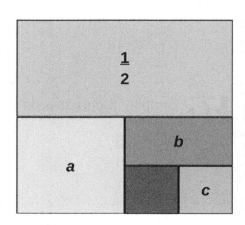

21. The rectangular prism shown has dimensions in inches. The prism will be completely filled with unit cubes that each have a volume of 1 cubic inch. How many of these cubes are needed to fill the prism?

A) 300

B) 325

C) 364

D) 388

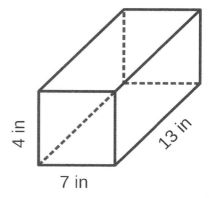

4 in

13 in

7 in

22. The rectangular prism shown has dimensions in feet. The rectangular prism will be completely filled with cubes with a volume of 8 cubic feet. How many of these cubes are needed to fill the prism?

A) 6

B) 9

C) 12

D) 72

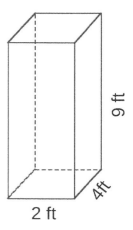

9 ft

4 ft

2 ft

23. A bakery ordered 150 loaves of bread for $2.50 each. What was the total cost of the bread?

A) $250

B) $375

C) $425

D) $500

13

24. Sarah needs to buy 12 notebooks. The bookstore sells the notebooks for $3.75 each. How much did Sarah spend on all the notebooks?

A) $45

B) $50

C) $62

D) $68

25. In which number is the digit 7 in the hundredths place? Select **two** correct answers.

A) 727.023

B) 1,350.0017

C) 4,523.172

D) 8,106.974

E) 9,700.367

26. The points on the grid represent values for $y = \frac{3}{4} x$. Which ordered pairs represent other points on the graph for this equation? Select **two** correct answers.

A) (3,4)

B) (4,3)

C) (9,0)

D) (0,12)

E) (8,6)

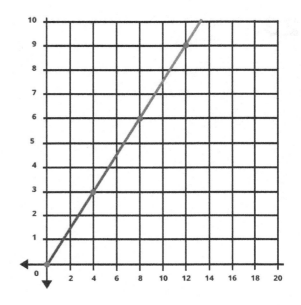

27. Jack's fishing rod is 175 inches long. What is the length of the fishing rod in feet?

(A) 13.5 ft

(B) 14.58 ft

(C) 0.15 ft

(D) 1,750 ft

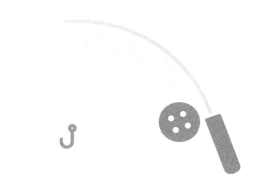

28. Tom's rectangular garden has a width of 70 in and a length of 50 in. What is the perimeter of Tom's garden in inches?

(A) 350 in

(B) 240 in

(C) 505 in

(D) 305 in

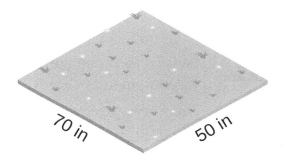

70 in   50 in

29. Which number is a composite number? Select **two** correct answers.

(A) 67

(B) 71

(C) 110

(D) 176

(E) 197

30. The values in the table represent the equation y = 3x – 2. Complete the table to represent the relationship between the values of x and y. Select the correct answer for each box. Each answer may be used more than once. Not all answers will be used.

Ⓐ 3
Ⓑ 11
Ⓒ 13
Ⓓ 25
Ⓔ 30
Ⓕ 34

x	y
5	A B C D E F
A B C D E F	7
9	A B C D E F
A B C D E F	31
12	A B C D E F

31. Jessica recorded the weights of five different boxes. The table displays four of her measurements:

Box	Weights
Box A	9.11
Box B	9.005
Box C	9.04
Box D	?
Box E	9.009

Box D has the second heaviest amount. Which of these options could represent the amount in Box D?

Ⓐ 9.009 Ⓑ 9.24 Ⓒ 9.09 Ⓓ 9.0099

16

32. What letter corresponds to the ordered pair (0,3)?

A) Point *M*

B) Point *L*

C) Point S

D) Point R

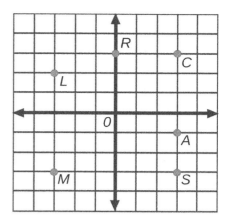

33. Where is point *A* located?

A) (7,2)

B) (2,6)

C) (2,7)

D) (-2,6)

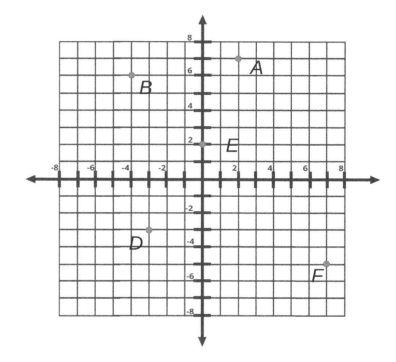

34. David practiced piano for 14.4 hours over the course of a week. He practiced for the same amount of time each day for 6 days. What was the total amount of time, in hours and minutes, he spent practicing each day?

A) 2 h 10 min

B) 2 h 24 min

C) 3 h 15 min

D) 3 h 36 min

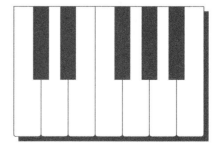

17

35. Maria baked cakes for a total of 10.5 hours over the course of 5 days. She spent the same amount of time baking each day. How many hours and minutes did she spend baking each day?

(A) 2 h 06 min

(B) 2 h 23 min

(C) 2 h 38 min

(D) 2 h 50 min

36. David's financial report for February revealed an income of $90 and expenses of $110. Which actions could David consider to balance his budget for February?

(A) Increase expenses and decrease income

(B) Increase expenses and increase income

(C) Decrease expenses and decrease income

(D) Decrease expenses and increase income

37. What is the value of the expression shown: $(5.24 \cdot 4 + 3.04) : 2 =$

(A) 10

(B) 12

(C) 14

(D) 16

18

38. An expression is shown $8\frac{1}{3} - 3 + 4\frac{1}{9} - 2\frac{2}{6}$. What is the value of the expression? Show your work.

39. Calculate and fill the blank rectangles with the correct decimal numbers.

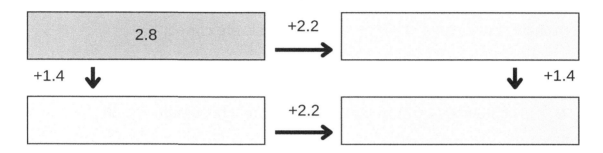

40. Emma bought 12 movie tickets for $90 in total. What was the cost of one movie ticket?

- (A) $6.5
- (B) $7.5
- (C) $8.5
- (D) $9.5

41. Sarah ran for 20 minutes every day for 5 days last week. This week, she ran for 25 minutes every day for 5 days. Which equation can be used to find m, the total number of minutes Sarah ran during these two weeks?

- (A) $m = (20 \cdot 5) + (25 \cdot 5)$
- (B) $m = (20 \cdot 5) - (25 \cdot 5)$
- (C) $m = (20 + 5) \cdot (25 + 5)$
- (D) $m = (20 + 5) + (25 + 5)$

42. Find the numerator of the fraction whose denominator is 24 and the value of the fraction is $\frac{1}{4}$. Show your work.

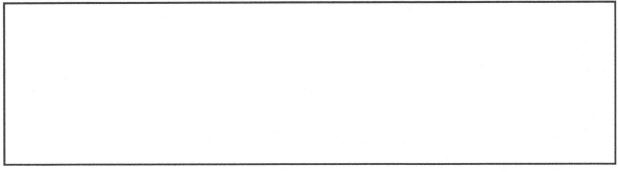

43. Which two statements about rounding decimals are correct?

(A) The number 4.067 rounded to the nearest hundredth is 4.07

(B) The number 4.071 rounded to the nearest hundredth is 4.08

(C) The number 4.116 rounded to the nearest hundredth is 4.10

(D) The number 4.108 rounded to the nearest hundredth is 4.11

(E) The number 4.025 rounded t the nearest hundredth is 4.02

44. In this right rectangular prism, each small cube measures 1 unit on each side. What is the volume of the prism?

(A) 90 cubic units

(B) 140 cubic units

(C) 190 cubic units

(D) 240 cubic units

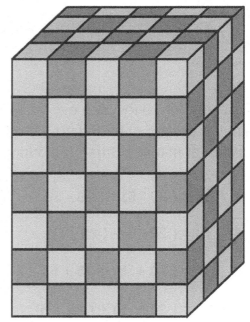

45. Which of these are all quadrilaterals?

- (A) Rectangle, square, triangle, trapezoid
- (B) Rectangle, trapezoid, square, parallelogram
- (C) Square, trapezoid, circle, rectangle
- (D) Pentagon, square, rectangle, parallelogram

46. Daniel is shown the coordinate grid with a point plotted.

He must plot a second point on the plane using the following rules:
Start at the plotted point. Subtract 4 from the x-coordinate. Add 5 to the y-coordinate.
Which ordered pair should Daniel plot on the grid?

- (A) (3,8)
- (B) (3,7)
- (C) (11,7)
- (D) (11,8)

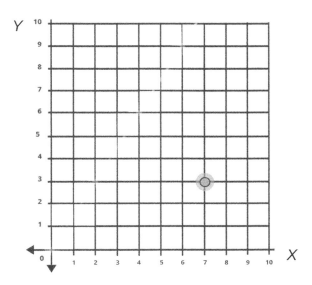

47. Look at the shapes below. Which shape has 90% of itself shaded?

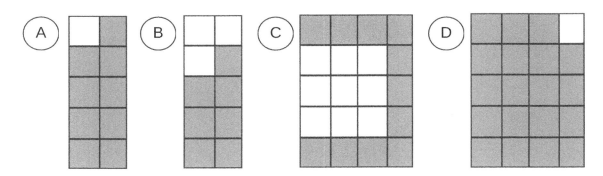

48. 35% of the class are girls. What percent are the boys?

A) 50%

B) 55%

C) 60%

D) 65%

49. Anna imagines some two-digit number. The sum of the digits of that number is 14. If we subtract 18 from that number, we will get the number which is written with the same digits but in reverse order. What is the number that Anna imagined?

A) 95

B) 86

C) 77

D) 68

50. The farmer had 100 eggs in a basket. He sold 15 eggs each day from Monday to Friday. How many eggs were left in the basket after selling eggs for five days?

A) 15

B) 20

C) 25

D) 30

Answers Test Practice 1

1. B, 6.75 cups of sugar
2. C and E, 1.04 and 1.0078
3. C, 6 ounces
4. D, 27
5. D, 23.8 F
6. B, Multiplicative pattern: each y-value is equals to x-value times 150
7. C, 9 square inches
8. A, 7.3 gallons
9. A, 18.8 gallons
10. A, 8.5 in
11. B, $\frac{6}{29}$
12. A, t = 180 - 25 - 70
13. A, $m = \frac{3}{4} - \frac{1}{3} - \frac{1}{6}$
14. B, 13
15. D, 3
16. A, 7
17. A, $\frac{5}{8}$
18. C, 1
19. D, $\frac{2}{9}$
20. A, $a = \frac{1}{4}$, $b = \frac{1}{8}$, $c = \frac{1}{16}$
21. C, 364
22. B, 9
23. B, $375
24. A, $45
25. C. 4,523.172 and D. 8,106.974
26. B and E, (4,3) and (8, 6)
27. B. 14.58 ft
28. B, 240 in
29. C and D, 110 and 176
30. C, A, D, B, F
31. C, 9.09
32. D, Point R
33. C, (2,7)
34. B, 2 h 24 min

35. A, 2 h 06 min
36. D, Decrease expenses and increase income
37. B, 12
38. $\frac{64}{9}$
39.

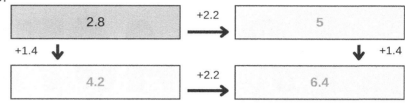

40. B, $7.5
41. A, $m = (20 \cdot 5) + (25 \cdot 5)$
42. 6
43. A and D, *4.067 rounded to the nearest hundredth is 4.07* and *4.108 rounded to the nearest hundredth is 4.11*
44. B, 140 cubic units
45. B, Rectangle, trapezoid, square, parallelogram
46. A, (3,8)
47. A,

48. D, 65%
49. B, 86
50. C, 25

PRACTICE TEST 2

GET STARTED →

1. The track team warms up for practice by jogging through the neighborhood near the school. A coordinate grid of the neighborhood is shown below:

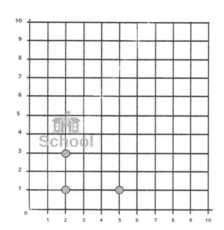

The team runs from the school along a path that forms a rectangle. Three of the vertices of the rectangle are shown on the grid. What are the coordinates of the fourth vertex of the rectangle?

A) (2, 5)

B) (3, 5)

C) (5, 3)

D) (5, 4)

2. Anna set a goal to swim 546 laps in her pool during summer vacation. She will swim 12 laps each day. What is the least whole number of days Anna will swim to reach her goal?

A) 45

B) 46

C) 47

D) 48

3. The three Smiths brothers are all 3 years apart in age. The total of their ages equals 33 years. What is the age of the oldest brother?

(A) 5

(B) 11

(C) 14

(D) 17

4. Sarah received a special award at the end of the school year. Her award, shown below, is a rectangular pyramid. Which of the following could be a top view of Sarah's award.

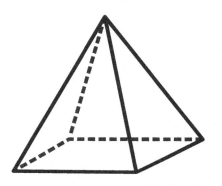

(A)

(B)

(C)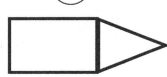

(D)

5. Side AC of the triangle measures 4 units and side BC measures 3 units.

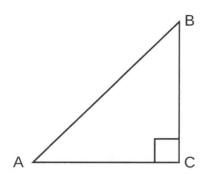

If you plot the triangle on a coordinate plane with point A at the origin (0, 0) and point C at (4, 0), what are the coordinates of point B?

(A) (3,4)

(B) (4,3)

(C) (2,3)

(D) (3,2)

6. The lowest known temperature for North pole was recorded in 1971. This temperature, in degrees Fahrenheit (°F), is represented by point *T* on the number line below:

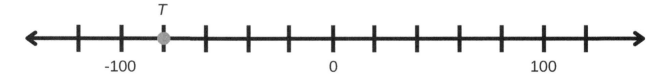

Which of the following temperatures, in °F, is higher than the temperature represented by point T?

(A) − 70°F

(B) − 80°F

(C) − 90°F

(D) − 100°F

27

7. In two days, David and James sold the same number of tickets to a festival. David sold 17 tickets on Monday and 30 tickets on Tuesday. James sold 22 tickets on Tuesday. Which equation can represent finding 's,' the number of tickets James sold on Monday?

(A) s = (17 + 30) − 22

(B) s = (17 + 30) + 22

(C) s = (17 − 30) − 22

(D) s = (17 + 30) + 22

8. Calculate and fill the blank rectangles with the correct decimal numbers:

231.042	+	1154.9	=	
+		+		
78.06	+	144.293	=	
=		=		
	+		=	

9. Christy wanted to find the surface area of a square pyramid. She wrote the expression shown below:

$(24 \cdot 5) : 2 + 6^2$

What is the value of the above expression?

- (A) 66
- (B) 76
- (C) 86
- (D) 96

10. A rectangle has an area of 100 square units.

Width = 5 Units

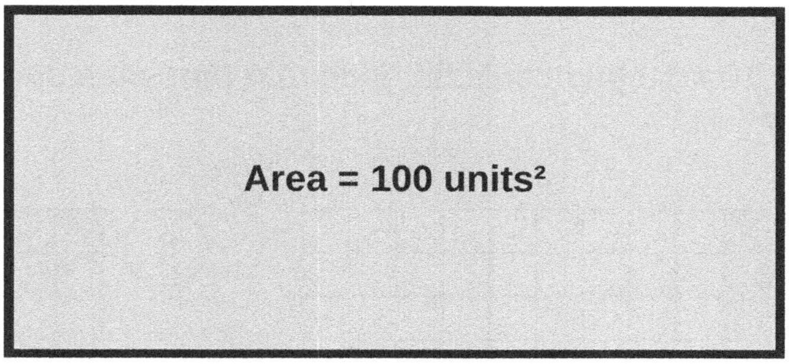

Area = 100 units²

Length = 20 Units

If the length is divided by 2, what must happen to the width for the area to remain the same?

- (A) The width must be increased by 50 units.
- (B) The width must be decreased by 50 units.
- (C) The width must be multiplied by 2.
- (D) The width must be divided by 2.

11. Tom has a puppy that is six months old. She has recorded the puppy's length in inches each month since it was one month old.

Month	January	February	March	April	May	June
Length (in inches)	14	18	19	22	25	28

Between which months did Tom's puppy grow the slowest?

(A) February and March

(B) March and April

(C) April and May

(D) May and June

12. Which 10 x 10 grid could be used to represent a decimal number equivalent to 0.030?

(A)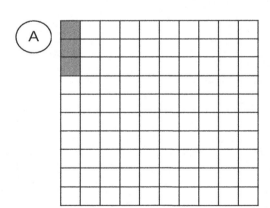

(B)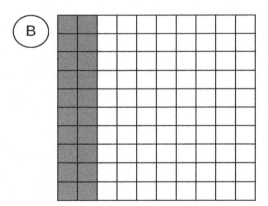

(C)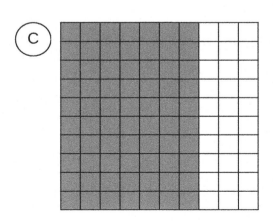

(D)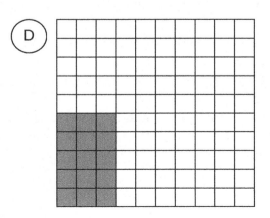

13. Which set of numbers is listed from least to greatest?

- (A) $0.5 ; 0.75 ; \frac{1}{4}$
- (B) $0.75 ; 0.5 ; \frac{1}{4}$
- (C) $\frac{1}{4} ; 0.5 ; 0.75$
- (D) $\frac{1}{4} ; 0.75 ; 0.5$

14. During a hailstorm, $\frac{1}{4}$ of the cars parked on a lot were dented. Which percent is equivalent to the fraction of cars that were dented?

- (A) 14%
- (B) 20%
- (C) 25%
- (D) 41%

15. Kerry went to the store and saw a sign that said, "Shirts are 25% off the regular price!" What is another way to say what the sign said?

- (A) Shirts are $\frac{1}{4}$ off the regular price.
- (B) Shirts are $\frac{1}{3}$ off the regular price.
- (C) Shirts are $\frac{3}{4}$ off the regular price.
- (D) Shirts are $\frac{1}{2}$ off the regular price.

16. Which list is in order from least to greatest?

(A) 8.120, 8.012, 8.201, 8.210

(B) 8.012, 8.120, 8.210, 8.201

(C) 8.012, 8.120, 8.201, 8.210

(D) 8.120, 8.201, 8.012, 8.201

17. What is the greatest common factor of 18 and 24?

(A) 2

(B) 3

(C) 4

(D) 6

18. The circle graph shows the results of a survey of 300 fifth-grade students to find out where they would like to go for their class field trip. How many students would like to go to the zoo?

(A) 75

(B) 90

(C) 100

(D) 125

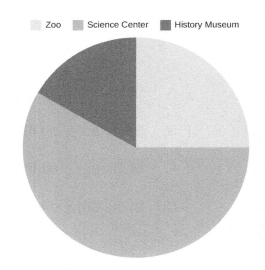

32

19. What is $10\frac{2}{3} - 8\frac{1}{7} + 6$?

- (A) $8\frac{11}{21}$
- (B) $11\frac{10}{21}$
- (C) $21\frac{10}{11}$
- (D) $21\frac{1}{10}$

20. Which solid object has 4 faces, 6 edges, and 4 vertices?

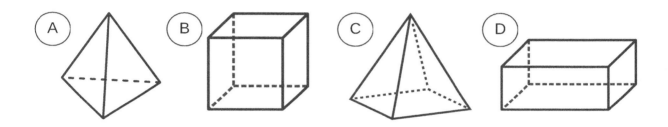

- (A)
- (B)
- (C)
- (D)

21. Five pounds of apples cost $5.78. Mary needs 10 pounds of apples to make applesauce. Which estimate is closest to the cost of 10 pounds of apples?

- (A) $10
- (B) $11
- (C) $12
- (D) $13

22. Use the picture below to answer the question.

What is the measure, in degrees, of the angle formed by the hands of the clock?

(A) 30°

(B) 45°

(C) 60°

(D) 90°

23. Select the two correct statements.

(A) The product of $\frac{3}{5}$ and 4 is greater than 4

(B) The product of $\frac{3}{5}$ and 4 is less than $\frac{3}{5}$

(C) The product of $1\frac{1}{2}$ and 2 is greater than $1\frac{1}{2}$

(D) The product of $1\frac{1}{2}$ and 2 is less than 2

(E) The product of $\frac{13}{4}$ and $\frac{5}{2}$ is greater than $\frac{13}{4}$

24. Knowing that the area of the square marked with a is twice the area of the square marked with b, and that $a + b + \frac{1}{3} = 1$ find the values of a and b.

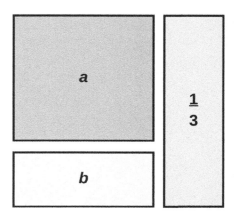

- (A) $a = \frac{4}{9}$, $b = \frac{2}{9}$
- (B) $a = \frac{1}{2}$, $b = \frac{1}{6}$
- (C) $a = \frac{2}{3}$, $b = \frac{1}{8}$
- (D) $a = \frac{1}{10}$, $b = \frac{3}{12}$

25. Consider the following table representing the relationship between the number of pages read (P) and the time spent reading (T) for a student:

The numbers that should correspond to the symbols * and # are:

- (A) * = 20, # = 2 hours
- (B) * = 30, # = 2 hours 30 minutes
- (C) * = 40, # = 2 hours
- (D) * = 35, # = 2 hours 45 minutes

Number of Pages Read	Time Spent Reading
0	0 Minutes
10	30 Minutes
*	1 Hour 30 Minutes
50	#
60	3 Hours

26. Jen makes a rectangular banner. It is $\frac{3}{4}$ yard long and $\frac{1}{4}$ yard wide. What is the area, in square yards, of the banner?

(A) 1

(B) 3

(C) $\frac{3}{8}$

(D) $\frac{3}{16}$

27. How many unit cubic boxes are contained within the box pictured below?

(A) 16

(B) 36

(C) 64

(D) 100

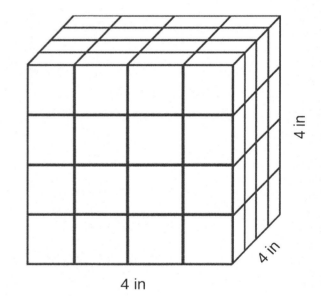

4 in

4 in

4 in

28. Emily measured her bamboo plant each day for 5 days. The table below shows the height of the plant each day:

Height of Bamboo Plant					
Day	1	2	3	4	5
Height (in inches)	10	12	13	15	17

Which of the following graphs can represent Emily's measurement data?

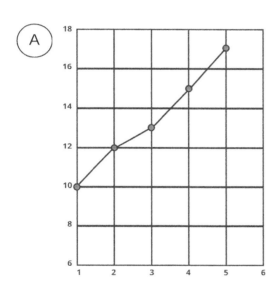

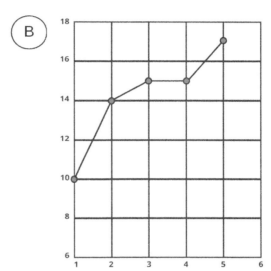

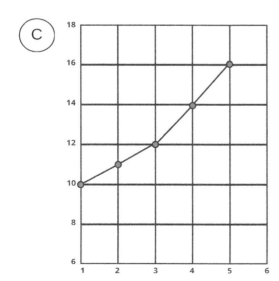

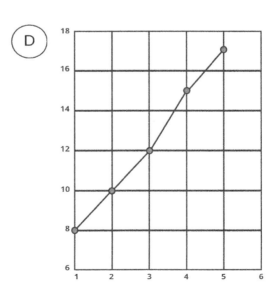

29. Which explanation about figures is correct?

(A) All rhombuses are parallelograms. Parallelograms have 2 pairs of parallel sides. Therefore, all rhombuses have 2 pairs of parallel sides.

(B) All rhombuses are parallelograms. Parallelograms have exactly 1 pair of parallel sides. Therefore, all rhombuses have exactly 1 pair of parallel sides.

(C) Only some rhombuses are parallelograms. Parallelograms have 2 pairs of parallel sides. Therefore, only some rhombuses have 2 pairs of parallel sides.

(D) Only some rhombuses are parallelograms. Parallelograms have exactly 1 pair of parallel sides. Therefore, only some rhombuses have exactly 1 pair of parallel sides.

30. On Saturday, Greg rode his bike $\frac{5}{8}$ of a mile. On Sunday, he rode his bike $\frac{1}{2}$ of a mile. Greg added $\frac{5}{8}$ and $\frac{1}{2}$ to find the total distance, in miles, he rode his bike on the two days.

Greg said $\frac{5}{8}$ + $\frac{1}{2}$ = $\frac{6}{10}$ and plotted on this number line

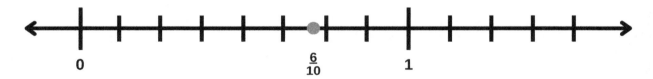

0          $\frac{6}{10}$ 1

(A) Explain why Greg's answer is not reasonable.

(B) Find the total distance, in miles, Greg rode on his bike on Saturday and Sunday

(C) Explain how to use the number line to show your answer is correct.

Show your answers below.

38

31. Tom read a quarter of the book on the first day, then two-thirds of what was left on the second day, and finally the last 40 pages on the third day. How many pages were there in the book?

- (A) 100 pages
- (B) 160 pages
- (C) 200 pages
- (D) 260 pages

32. The father is now three times older than the son. In 12 years, the father will be twice as old as the son. How old is the father now, and how old is the son?

- (A) Son = 10 years, Father = 30 years
- (B) Son = 12 years, Father = 36 years
- (C) Son = 14 years, Father = 42 years
- (D) Son = 16 years, Father = 48 years

33. In a survey of students' favorite colors, the results were as follows: 25% chose blue, 30% chose red, 20% chose green, and the rest chose yellow. If 60 students participated in the survey, how many students chose yellow as their favorite color?

- (A) 5
- (B) 10
- (C) 15
- (D) 20

34. Which cube has a volume of 438.976 cubic inches?

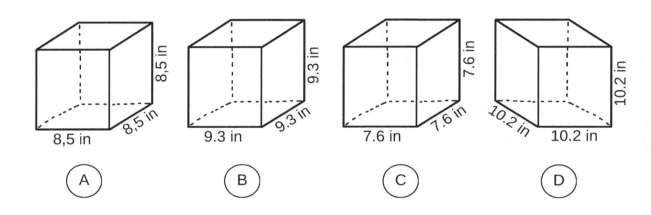

8,5 in   8,5 in   8,5 in   (A)

9.3 in   9.3 in   9.3 in   (B)

7.6 in   7.6 in   7.6 in   (C)

10.2 in   10.2 in   10.2 in   (D)

35. Simplify the expression $(16\frac{2}{5} \cdot 2.5 - 4\frac{4}{5}):4.5 =$

- (A) 7
- (B) 7.23
- (C) 8
- (D) 8.04

40

36. Simplify the expression $(48 : 6\frac{2}{5} - 1\frac{1}{4}) : \frac{5}{8} =$

- (A) 8.5
- (B) 9
- (C) 10
- (D) 12

37. What fraction, with a denominator of 9, is greater than $\frac{2}{3}$ and less than $\frac{5}{6}$?

- (A) $\frac{1}{9}$
- (B) $\frac{4}{9}$
- (C) $\frac{7}{9}$
- (D) $\frac{12}{9}$

38. An expression is given.

$5 (3^2 + 56 : 8) - 4 (3.5)$

What is the value of this expression?

- (A) 56
- (B) 60
- (C) 66
- (D) 70

39. A baker used a total of 1.8 ounces of dough to make 12 equally sized loaves of bread. How much dough in ounces was used for each loaf of bread?

A) 0.1 oz

B) 0.15 oz

C) 0.23 oz

D) 0.275 oz

40. Thomas is a car salesman. The table shows the salary that Thomas earns for the number of cars he sells.

Number of Cars Sold	Monthly Salary Earned
0	$2200
1	$2800
2	$3400
3	$4000
4	$4600

Which graph represents Thomas's data, and what does the slope signify?

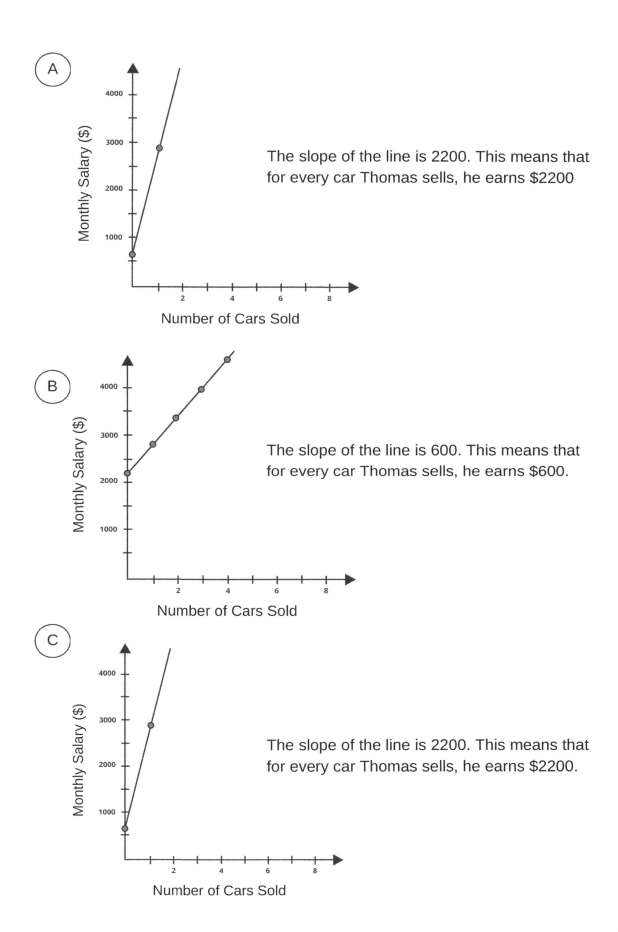

A

The slope of the line is 2200. This means that for every car Thomas sells, he earns $2200

B

The slope of the line is 600. This means that for every car Thomas sells, he earns $600.

C

The slope of the line is 2200. This means that for every car Thomas sells, he earns $2200.

43

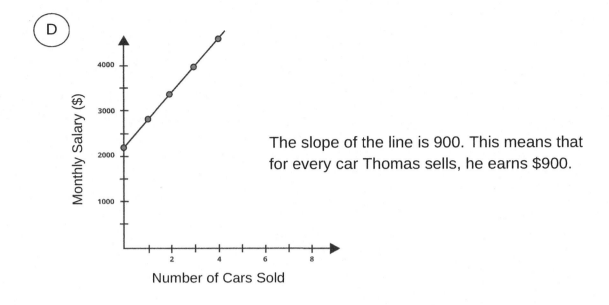

The slope of the line is 900. This means that for every car Thomas sells, he earns $900.

41. Each block on the tower shown measures 4 cubic in in volume. What is the total volume of the tower?

(A) 4 cubic in

(B) 10 cubic in

(C) 40 cubic in

(D) 100 cubic in

42. If a clock shows 7:45 AM, what is approximately the measure of the angle between the hour and minute hands?

- (A) 45°
- (B) 90°
- (C) 120°
- (D) 180°

43. What is the perimeter of a regular hexagon with each side measuring 4 in?

- (A) 20 in
- (B) 24 in
- (C) 28 in°
- (D) 32 in

44. Which of the following numbers is a composite number?

- (A) 11
- (B) 13
- (C) 17
- (D) 21

45. If point A has coordinates (4,0) and point B has coordinates (0, 3), what is the distance between A and B?

- (A) 3 units
- (B) 4 units
- (C) 5 units
- (D) 10 units

46. A triangle has vertices at coordinates (2, 1), (6, 3), and (4, 7). What type of triangle is it?

- (A) Equilateral
- (B) Isosceles
- (C) Scalene
- (D) Right-angled

47. Which two conversions are correct?

- (A) 7 in = 70 ft
- (B) 7 in = 0.583 ft
- (C) 7,000 yd = 3.98 miles
- (D) 7 miles = 7852 yd

48. An expression is given.

$$\left(\frac{1}{8} \left(2\frac{1}{4} : 1\frac{1}{2} \right) + 3 \right) : \left(1 - \frac{1}{8} \right)$$

What is the value of this expression? Show your work.

49. One swimming pool contains 2693 gallons of water. The pool is 15 feet long and 12 feet wide. What is the depth of the pool? Show your work.

50. During the first week, Tom ran for x minutes each day for n days. During the second week, he increased his running time to y minutes each day for the same n days. Which equation can be used to find m, the total number of minutes Tom ran during these two weeks?

- (A) $m = x \cdot n + y : n$
- (B) $m = (x + y) \cdot n$
- (C) $m = x \cdot y \cdot n$
- (D) $m = x \cdot n + y : n$

Answers Test Practice 2

1. C, (5,3)
2. B, 46
3. C, 14
4. D,
5. B, (4,3)
6. A, – 70°F
7. A, s = (17 + 30) – 22
8.

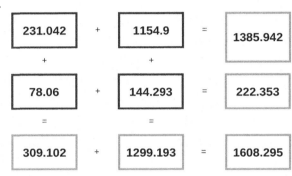

231.042	+	1154.9	=	1385.942
+		+		
78.06	+	144.293	=	222.353
=		=		
309.102	+	1299.193	=	1608.295

9. D, 96
10. C, The width must be multiplied by 2.
11. A, February and March
12. A,

13. C, $\frac{1}{4}$; 0.5 ; 0.75
14. C, 25%
15. A, Shirts are 1/4 off the regular price.
16. C, 8.012, 8.120, 8.201, 8.210
17. D, 6
18. A, 75 students would like to go to the zoo.
19. A, $8\frac{11}{21}$

20. A,
21. C, $12
22. C, 60°
23. C and E
24. A, $a = \frac{4}{9}$, $b = \frac{2}{9}$
25. B, * = 30, # =2 hours 30 minutes
26. D, 3/16 square yards.
27. C, 64

28. A

29. A, All rhombuses are parallelograms. Parallelograms have 2 pairs of parallel sides. Therefore, all rhombuses have 2 pairs of parallel sides.

30. a) Greg's answer is not reasonable because he added fractions with different denominators, which means he added the numerators with numerators with numerators and denominators to denominators, which is incorrect. He should have added the fractions with the same denominator.

b) To find the total distance Greg rode on his bike on Saturday and Sunday, we need to add the fractions 5/8 miles and ½ miles = 1.125 miles

$$\frac{5}{8} + \frac{1}{2} = \frac{5+4}{8} = \frac{9}{8} = 1\frac{1}{8}$$

c)

31. B, 160 pages
32. B, 12 years old and the father is 36 years old.
33. C, 15 students chose yellow as their favorite color
34. C, 7.6 in
35. D, 8.04
36. C, 10
37. C, 7/9 is greater than 2/3 and less than 5/6
38. C, 66
39. B, 0.15 of dough was used for each loaf of bread.
40. B, The slope of the line is 600. This means that for every car Thomas sells, he earns $600.
41. C, 40 cubic in
42. A, 45°
43. B, 24 in
44. D, 21
45. C, 5 units
46. B, Isosceles.
47. B and C, 7 in = 0.583 ft and 7,000 yd = 3.98 miles
48. 8.5
49. 2 ft
50. B, m = (x + y) · n

48

PRACTICE TEST 3

GET STARTED →

1. Mr. Frank wants to fence his backyard with three rows of wire fences. The dimensions of his backyard are given in the picture. How many ft of wire fences does Mr. Frank need to fence his backyard?

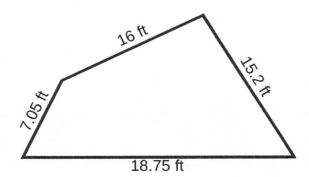

16 ft

15.2 ft

7.05 ft

18.75 ft

(A) 160 ft

(B) 171 ft

(C) 210 ft

(D) 300 ft

2. Calculate and fill the blank rectangles with the correct decimal numbers:

562.3	-	98.72	=	

|
|

58.595	-	5.938	=	

=
=

	-		=	

3. An expression is given.

$$\left(1\tfrac{2}{5} + 3.5 : \tfrac{1}{4}\right) : 2\tfrac{2}{5} + 3.4 : 2\tfrac{1}{8} - 0.35$$

What is the value of this expression? Show your work.

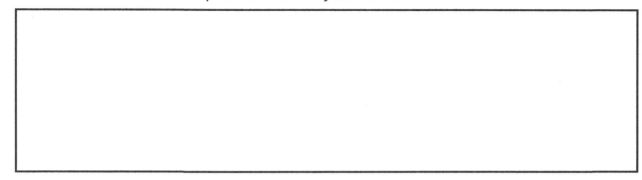

4. Maggie is shown the coordinate grid with a point plotted.

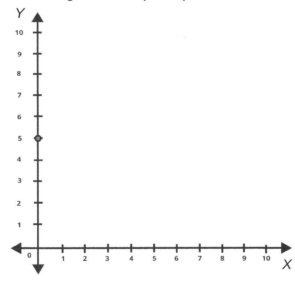

She must plot a second point on the plane using the following rules:
Start at the plotted point. Add 3 to the x-coordinate. Add 2 to the y-coordinate.
Which ordered pair should Maggie plot on the grid?

A) (8, 2)

B) (3, 7)

C) (2, 3)

D) (3, 3)

5. Select the two equations that are correct when the number 200 is entered in place of the symbol *

(A) * · 85 = 17,000

(B) * : 40 = 50

(C) 15,000 : * = 75

(D) 1,200 · 6 = *

(E) * · 50 = 1,000

6. An egg farm packages 264 total cartons of eggs each month. The farm has 3 different sizes of cartons.

- The small carton holds 8 eggs and $\frac{1}{6}$ of total cartons are small.
- The medium carton holds 12 eggs and $\frac{2}{3}$ of the total cartons are medium.
- The large carton holds 18 eggs and the rest of the total cartons are large.

Determine how many of each size of carton is needed each month. Then determine how many eggs are needed to fill the 264 cartons.

Show your work or explain your answers.

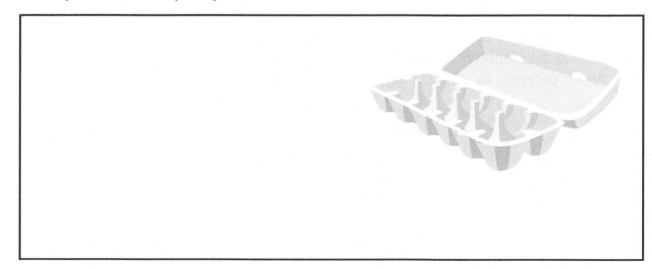

7. Select the two statements that correctly describe the point plotted on the coordinate plane:

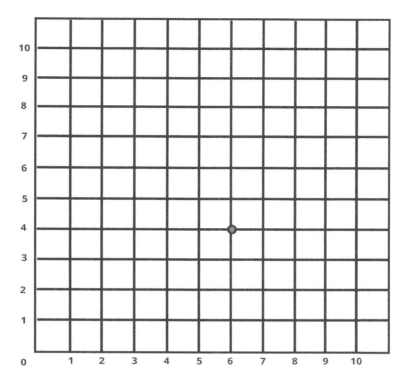

A) The point is located at the ordered pair (4, 6)

B) The point is located at the ordered pair (6, 4)

C) The x-coordinate is 4 and the y – coordinate is 6

D) The point is 4 units t the right of the origin on the x-axis and 6 units up from the origin on the y-axis'

E) The point is 6 units to the right of the origin on the x-axis and 4 units up from the origin on the y-axis.

8. David drew a rectangular maze with a length of $\frac{3}{4}$ foot and a width of $\frac{5}{12}$ foot. What is the area, in square feet, of David's maze?

- (A) $\frac{15}{48}$
- (B) $\frac{8}{16}$
- (C) $\frac{20}{60}$
- (D) $\frac{15}{16}$

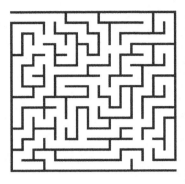

9. Kate brought a basket of eggs to the market. The first buyer bought half of the total number of eggs and half an egg more. The second buyer bought half of the remaining eggs and half an egg more. The third buyer was served in the same way, as were the other two, and the fourth buyer too. Then the basket remained empty. How many eggs did Kate bring to the market?

- (A) 10 eggs
- (B) 15 eggs
- (C) 20 eggs
- (D) 25 eggs

10. During a semester, a student received scores of 76, 80, 83, 71, 80, and 78 on six tests. What is the student's average score for these six tests?

- (A) 76
- (B) 77
- (C) 78
- (D) 79

54

11. On the three sections of a math test, a student correctly answered the number of questions shown in the table above. What percent of the questions on the entire test did the student answer correctly?

Section	Total Number of Questions	Number of Questions Answered Correctly
Algebra	20	17
Data Analysis	15	11
Geometry	25	20

- (A) 20%
- (B) 48%
- (C) 75%
- (D) 80%

12. Ms. Smith needs to order rope for her gym class of 32 students. Each student will receive a piece of rope that is 5 feet 8 inches long. What is the total length of rope Ms. Smith needs to order for her class?

- (A) 106 feet 8 inches
- (B) 154 feet 8 inches
- (C) 160 feet 8 inches
- (D) 181 feet 4 inches

13. Peter works 38 hours per week and earns $7.25 per hour. His employer gives him a raise that increases his weekly gross pay to $307.80. What is the increase in Peter's weekly gross pay?

- Ⓐ $32.30
- Ⓑ $34.70
- Ⓒ $42.46
- Ⓓ $275.50

14. The table shows Sarah's grades for a class.

Quiz Average	Test Average	Final Exam
83%	79%	88%

For her overall average, the test average counts twice as much as the quiz average, and the final exam counts twice as much as the test average. To find her overall average, Sarah uses the following expression:

(83 + 79 + 79 + 88 + 88 + 88 + 88) : 7

Which of the following is another way to find her overall average?

- Ⓐ $83 + 2 \cdot \frac{79}{7} + 4 \cdot \frac{88}{7}$
- Ⓑ $83 + 0.2 \cdot 79 + 0.4 \cdot 88$
- Ⓒ $(83 + 2 \cdot 79 + 4 \cdot 88) : 0.7$
- Ⓓ $(83 + 2 \cdot 79 + 4 \cdot 88) \cdot \frac{1}{7}$

56

15. The chart below displays a relationship between values of x and y. given this relationship, what would be the value of y that is missing?

- A) 5
- B) 6.5
- C) 7
- D) 7.5

X	Y
1	3
1.5	4.5
2	6
2.5	
3	9
3.5	10.5

16. The graph shows the sales of a commodity over a 20-year period. Between what years did sales increase by the greatest amount?

- A) Between 2004 and 2009
- B) Between 2009 and 2014
- C) Between 2014 and 2019
- D) Between 2019 and 2024

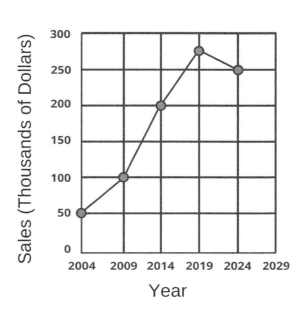

17. The total land area for one country is 3,537,438 square miles. What is this value rounded to the nearest thousand square miles?

(A) 3,500,000 square miles

(B) 3,537,000 square miles

(C) 3,538,000 square miles

(D) 3,540,000 square miles

18. Which point represents (5, 2) on this graph?

(A) Point K

(B) Point L

(C) Point M

(D) Point N

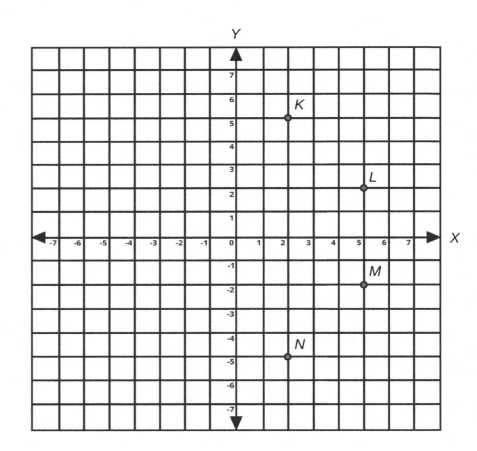

19. If you append 9 to a certain number from the right side, divide by 13 from the resulting number, then to the quotient obtained append 1 from the right side, and divide the resulting number by 11, the result is 21. What is that number?

- (A) 29
- (B) 34
- (C) 58
- (D) 61

20. Tina scored the following numbers for points in five dart games:

88, 96, 112, 135, 144

What is the median of these numbers?

- (A) 56
- (B) 88
- (C) 112
- (D) 115

21. The measures of three interior angles in a quadrilateral are 35°, 50° and 125°. What is the degree measure of the fourth interior angle?

- (A) 60°
- (B) 90°
- (C) 120°
- (D) 150°

22. Nana made a triangle by cutting the corner off a sheet of paper.

One angle is 45°. What is the measure of the third angle of Nana's triangle?

 A 30°

 B 45°

C 55°

D 60°

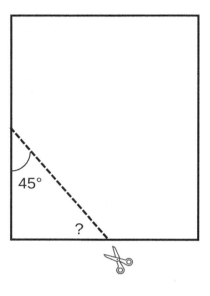

45°

?

23. A store has a rectangular parking lot that is 100 feet by 125.5 feet. What is the perimeter of parking lot?

 **A** 220 feet

B 360 feet

C 451 feet

D 12,000 feet

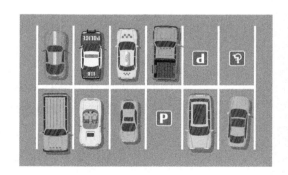

60

24. What is the volume, in cubic yards, of the storage unit below?

- (A) 11
- (B) 30.5
- (C) 40.5
- (D) 47.25

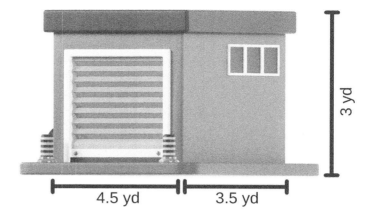

3 yd

4.5 yd   3.5 yd

25. What is the surface area of the box formed by the pattern below?

- (A) 28 square in
- (B) 24 square in
- (C) 14 square in
- (D) 8 square in

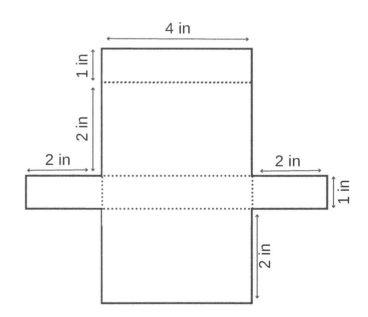

4 in

1 in

2 in

2 in   2 in

1 in

2 in

26. The vertices of a triangle are represented by the ordered pairs (0, 3), (3, 7) and (6, 4). Which of the following shows the vertices of the triangle?

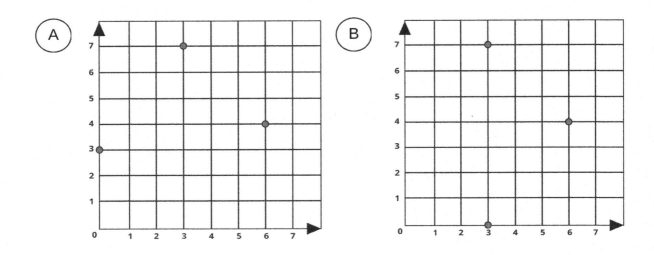

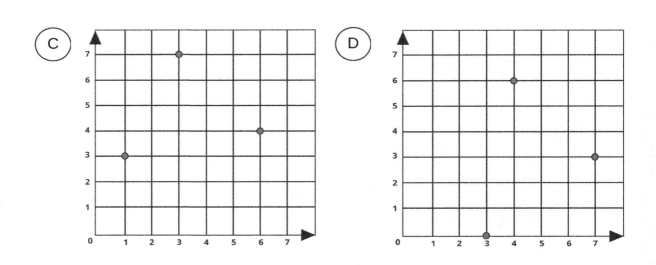

27. Which of the following shows the number 15.8362 rounded to the hundredth?

(A) 15.83

(B) 15.84

(C) 15.836

(D) 15.837

28. An expression is given.

$(12 \cdot 5 - 39) + 2 (75 - 15 \cdot 5) - 20$

What is the value of this expression?

(A) 0

(B) 1

(C) 2

(D) 12

29. Sarah is baking a cake using a recipe that requires $\frac{2}{3}$ cup of sugar. However, she decides to make half of the recipe, so she needs to adjust the amount of sugar accordingly. Additionally, the recipe calls for $\frac{1}{4}$ cup of butter, which Sarah knows is equivalent to 0.25 cups. After carefully measuring the ingredients, Sarah realizes she only has 0.4 kilograms of sugar left in her pantry. She needs to convert this amount to cups to determine if she has enough sugar for the cake. If 1 kilogram is equal to approximately 4.2 cups of sugar, does Sarah have enough sugar to make the cake?

- (A) There's not enough information to answer the question.
- (B) No, Sarah does not have enough sugar.
- (C) Sarah has exactly enough sugar.
- (D) Sarah has more sugar than needed.

30. Emily is planning a party and wants to make fruit punch for her guests. The recipe calls for $\frac{3}{4}$ gallon of fruit juice. However, Emily realizes she only has 0.6 liters of fruit juice available. If 1 gallon is equal to approximately 3.785 liters, does Emily have enough fruit juice to make the punch?

- (A) There's not enough information to answer the question.
- (B) No, Emily does not have enough fruit juice.
- (C) Emily has exactly enough fruit juice.
- (D) Emily has more fruit juice than needed.

31. James is building a rectangular garden bed in his backyard. He wants the length to be $\frac{5}{6}$ ft and the width to be $\frac{3}{4}$ ft. If he has a total of 18 square ft of area available for the garden bed, will the garden bed fit in the available space?

- (A) Yes, the garden bed will fit in the available space.
- (B) No, the garden bed will not fit in the available space.
- (C) The garden bed exactly fits in the available space.
- (D) There is not enough information to determine if the garden bed will fit.

32. Sarah is filling a rectangular fish tank with water. The tank has a length of 1.5 ft, a width of 1 ft, and a height of 0.8 ft. If she fills the tank to a height of 0.6 ft, how many gallons of water will the tank hold?

- (A) 4.509 gallons
- (B) 5.022 gallons
- (C) 6.732 gallons
- (D) 9.055 gallons

33. John is recording the outcomes of his chess games for the past month. He played a total of 20 games and won 12 of them. What percentage of his games did John win?

- (A) 60%
- (B) 55%
- (C) 65%
- (D) 70%

65

34. Mrs. Watson makes study guides for her class of 21 students. She uses 252 sheets of paper. How many sheets of paper are in each study guide?

(A) 12 sheets

(B) 24 sheets

(C) 30 sheets

(D) 38 sheets

35. Which picture shows 180° of a circle?

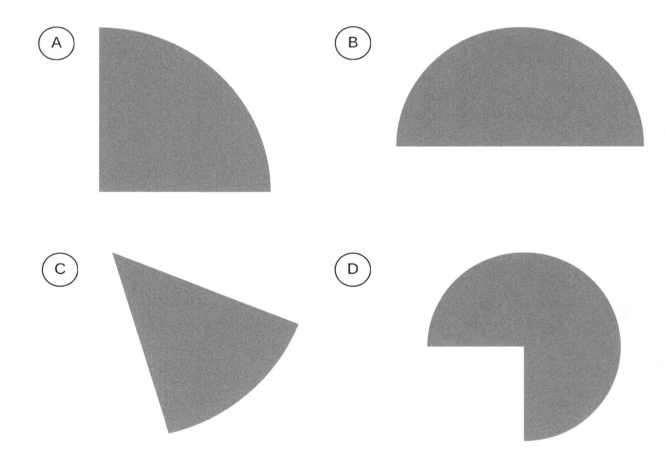

(A)

(B)

(C)

(D)

36. Each time John goes to the movies he spends $7.00. Which expression shows how much he spends after going to the movies t times?

- (A) t + $7
- (B) t : $7
- (C) t · $7
- (D) t − $7

37. Select the two statements that correctly describe the coordinate system.

- (A) The origin is located at (0, 0).
- (B) The x- and y-axes do not intersect.
- (C) The x- and y- axes are intersecting number lines.
- (D) The value of the y-coordinate is the first number in an ordered pair.
- (E) The value of the x-coordinate is the second number in an ordered pair.

38. Which equations shows the relationship of all values in the table below?

- (A) y = 3x
- (B) x = 3y
- (C) y = x + 3
- (D) x = y + 3

X	Y
-2	-6
-1	-3
0	0
1	3
2	6

39. If s = 4, what is the value of s (9 − 4) ?

(A) 16

(B) 20

(C) 32

(D) 45

40. Sophie caught twice as many fish as her dad. If her dad caught F fish, how many fish did Sophie catch.

(A) F + 2

(B) F − 2

(C) F · 2

(D) F : 2

41. The table shows the height of an elevator above ground level after a certain amount of time. Model the data with a line graph. Let y represent the height of the elevator in feet, and let x represent the time in seconds.

Time (s)	Height (ft)
10	202
20	186
40	196
60	200

42. A rectangular prism has dimensions of length 6 units, width 4 units, and height 3 units. How many cubic boxes with side length 1 unit can be contained within this prism?

(A) 72

(B) 24

(C) 12

(D) 10

43. Sophia is training for a marathon and records her daily running distance. Last week, she ran 5 miles each day for 7 days. This week, she ran 10% more than 5 miles each day. How much more total distance does Sophia cover this week compared to last week?

(A) 3 miles

(B) 3.5 miles

(C) 4 miles

(D) 4.5 miles

44. Kyrie has a bag filled with 100 jelly beans. In the bag, 15 of the jelly beans are red. Select the expression that represent the portion of the jelly beans that are red.

(A) 100 − 15

(B) 100 + 15

(C) 100 : 15

(D) 15 : 100

45. A line plot shows the numbers of points scored by all the players on both teams during a basketball game.

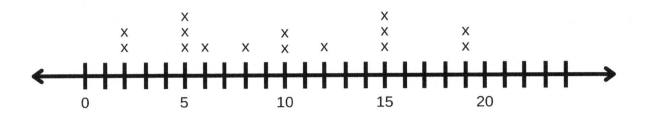

What is the median number of points scored?

- (A) 10
- (B) 19
- (C) 20
- (D) 21

46. Order these numbers 14.747; 14.447; 14.744; 14.477; 14.474 from greatest to least.

- (A) 14.447; 14.474; 14.477; 14.744; 14.747
- (B) 14.744; 14.747; 14.474; 14.477; 14.447
- (C) 14.747; 14.744; 14.474; 14.477; 14.447
- (D) 14.747; 14.744; 14.477; 14.474; 14.447

47. The table below represents a relationship between the number of months (x) and the amount of money saved (y) in a savings account

X	Y
1.5	364.5
3	729
4.5	1093.5
6	1458

Which statement about the relationship between the number of months (x) and the amount of money saved (y) is true?

A) It is a multiplicative pattern because each y-value is given by it's corresponding x-value times 143.

B) It is a multiplicative pattern because each y-value is given by it's corresponding x-value times 243.

C) It is an additive pattern because each y-value can be determined by adding 364.5 to the corresponding x-value.

D) IIt is an additive pattern because each y-value can be determined by adding 264.5 to the corresponding x-value.

48. Mr. Ben is building a concrete patio in his backyard. The patio will measure 1 foot deep by 12 feet wide by 15 feet long. If concrete costs $4/cubic foot, how much will Mr. Ben need to pay for the concrete for his patio?

A) $112

B) $180

C) $288

D) $720

49. If 2X + 3 = 11, what is the value of 4X + 6 ?

- (A) 20
- (B) 22
- (C) 24
- (D) 26

50. Jose is packing cube-shaped blocks in the box shown

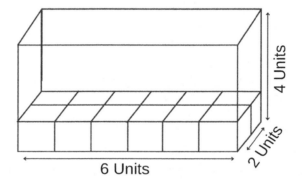

Which two expressions could be used to calculate the volume of the box, in cubic units?

- (A) 6 · 2 · 4
- (B) 6 + 2 + 4
- (C) 12 · 4
- (D) 12 + 4

Answers Practice Test 3

1.B, 171 ft

2.

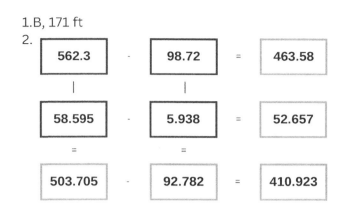

3.Answer is 23/3.

4.B, (3, 7)

5.A and C, * · 85 = 17,000 and 15,000 : * = 75

6.Small = 44, medium = 176, large = 44 / total number of eggs = 3256

7.B and E, *The point is located at the ordered pair (6, 4)* and *The point is 6 units to the right of the origin on the x-axis and 4 units up from the origin on the y-axis.*

8.A, $\frac{15}{48}$

9.B, 15

10.C, 78

11.D, 80%

12.D, 181 feet 4 inches

13.A, $32.30

14.D, $(83 + 2 \cdot 79 + 4 \cdot 88) \cdot \frac{1}{7}$

15.D, 7.5

16.B, Between 2009 and 2014

17.B, 3,537,000 square miles

18.B, Point L

19.A, 29

20.C, 112

21.D, 150°

22.B, 45°

23.C, 451 feet

24.D, 47.25

25.A, 28 square in

26.A,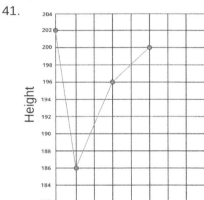

27.B, 15.84

28.B, 1

29.D, Sarah has more sugar than needed.

30.B, No, Emily does not have enough fruit juice.

31.A, Yes, the garden bed will fit in the available space.

32.C, 6.732 gallons

33.A, 60%

34.A, 12 sheets

35.B, The half of circle is 180 degrees.

36.C, t · $7

37.A and C,*The origin is located at (0, 0)* and *The x- and y- axes are intersecting number lines.*

38.A, y = 3x

39.B, 20

40.C, F · 2

41.

42.A, 72

43.B, 3.5 miles

44.D, 15: 100

45.A, 10

46.D, 14.747; 14.744; 14.477; 14.474; 14.447

47.B, It is a multiplicative pattern because each y-value is given by its corresponding x-value times 243.

48.D, $720

49.B, 22

50.A and C, 6 · 2 · 4 and 12 · 4

PRACTICE TEST 4

GET STARTED →

1. Which cube has an area of 518.94 squared inches?

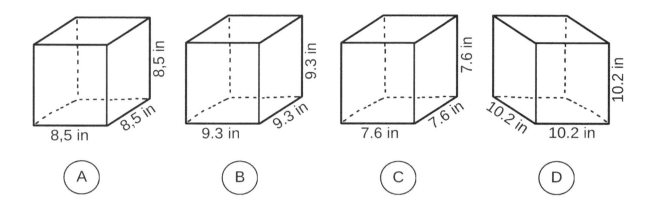

2. Look at the shapes below. Which shape has 70% of its area not shaded?

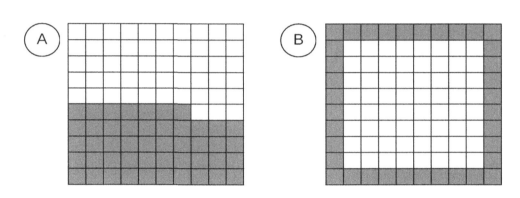

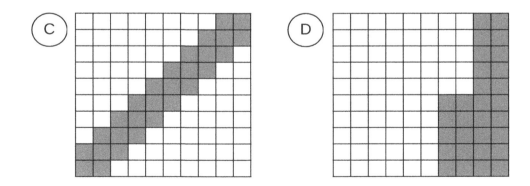

3. Jacob is creating a map of his neighborhood on a coordinate plane. His apartment is located at point (5, 0) on the coordinate plane. Now, he plots the location of the post office on the coordinate plane. He graphs it 4 units to the right and 2 units up from his apartment. What is the coordinate pair that represents the location of the post office?

A) (1, 2)

B) (2, 4)

C) (4, 7)

D) (9, 2)

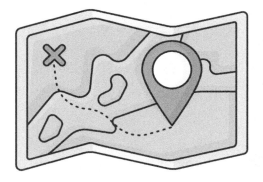

4. Tina wants to buy 1 dozen cookies (12 cookies). What is the difference in price between buying 12 cookies individually and buying them by the dozen?

A) 0.2

B) 0.4

C) 0.6

D) 2.4

Cookies

20¢ each or $2.00 per dozen

5. A bag contains the 26 letters of the alphabet on individual tiles. What is the probability of randomly drawing an A or Z out of the bag?

A) $\frac{1}{26}$

B) $\frac{1}{13}$

C) $\frac{1}{12}$

D) $\frac{1}{2}$

6. Which table matches the information on the graph?

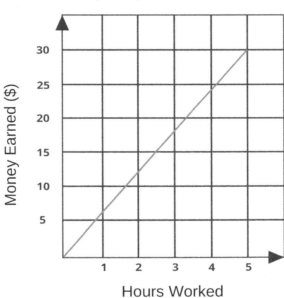

Hourly Wages for Summer Jobs

A)

Hours Worked	1	2	3	4	5
Money Earned	$6	$12	$18	$24	$30

(B)	Hours Worked	1	2	3	4	5
	Money Earned	$5	$10	$20	$25	$30

(C)	Hours Worked	1	2	3	4	5
	Money Earned	$5	$10	$15	$20	$25

(D)	Hours Worked	1	2	3	4	5
	Money Earned	$7	$14	$21	$28	$35

7. The line graph shows Christina's heart rate at 5-minute intervals after she starts exercising.

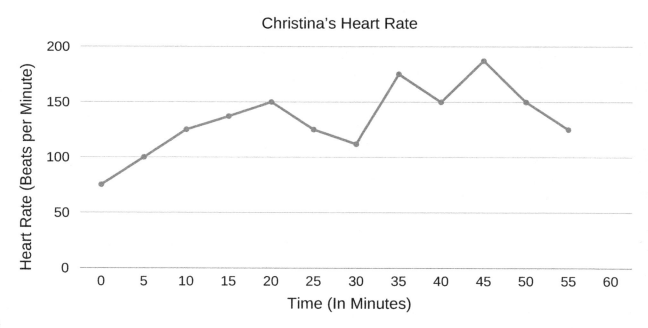

Christina's Heart Rate

During which 5-minute interval did Christina's heart rate increase the most?

A) 15 minutes to 20 minutes

B) 30 minutes to 35 minutes

C) 40 minutes to 45 minutes

D) 45 minutes to 50 minutes

8. Adam walks $\frac{3}{10}$ mile in the morning to school. He walks $\frac{2}{5}$ mile in the afternoon to a friend's house. Adam says that he walks a total of $\frac{5}{15}$ mile in the morning and afternoon. Which two statement are true?

A) Since $\frac{3}{10}$ plus $\frac{2}{5}$ is $\frac{5}{15}$, the total of $\frac{5}{15}$ is reasonable

B) Since $\frac{5}{15}$ is less than $\frac{2}{5}$, the total of $\frac{5}{15}$ is not reasonable

C) The fractions $\frac{5}{15}$, $\frac{3}{10}$ and $\frac{2}{5}$ are all less than $\frac{1}{4}$ so the total of $\frac{5}{15}$ is reasonable

D) The fraction $\frac{5}{15}$ is $\frac{1}{3}$ and $\frac{1}{3}$ is greater than $\frac{3}{10}$. Since $\frac{5}{15}$ is greater than one of the addends, the total of $\frac{5}{15}$ is reasonable

E) The fractions $\frac{3}{10}$ and $\frac{2}{5}$ are each greater than $\frac{1}{4}$ so the total must be greater than $\frac{1}{2}$. The fraction $\frac{5}{15}$ is less than $\frac{1}{2}$, so the total of is $\frac{5}{15}$ not reasonable.

9. What is 75% of 40?

A) 10

B) 20

C) 30

D) 40

10. Simplify the expression: $8\frac{1}{9} + 4\frac{1}{10} - 8\frac{4}{15}$

(A) $\frac{1}{18}$

(B) $\frac{17}{18}$

(C) $3\frac{17}{18}$

(D) $4\frac{1}{18}$

11. What decimal is equal to: $\frac{3}{5}$

(A) 0.35

(B) 0.40

(C) 0.55

(D) 0.60

12. What is $\frac{3}{8}$ written as a percent?

(A) 26.7%

(B) 30%

(C) 37.5%

(D) 42%

13. The rectangle and the square have equal perimeters. The length of the side of the square is 7 inches, and the length of the side of the rectangle is 4 inches greater than its width. Calculate the lengths of the sides of the rectangle.

14. Simplify the expression $(7.6 \cdot 3.4) + 5.2$

- (A) 31.04
- (B) 36.56
- (C) 38.52
- (D) 41.68

15. If $X = \frac{3}{4}$ and $Y = \frac{5}{6}$, what is the value of $\frac{Y}{X} - \frac{X}{Y}$?

- (A) $\frac{19}{100}$
- (B) $\frac{19}{90}$
- (C) $2\frac{19}{100}$
- (D) $3\frac{19}{90}$

16. If n – 4 = 12, what is the value of 2n + 5?

- (A) 29
- (B) 33
- (C) 37
- (D) 41

17. What is the value of 2(3x – 4) – (5x + 2), when x = 7?

- (A) -3
- (B) -10
- (C) 12
- (D) 20

18. What is the volume of rectangular prism with dimensions 5.2in by 10.4in by 7.8in?

- (A) 420.825 square inches
- (B) 421.824 square inches
- (C) 482.221 square inches
- (D) 484.121 square inches

19. In a survey, 80% of students preferred pizza, 10% preferred burgers, and the rest preferred tacos. If there were 120 students surveyed, how many preferred tacos?

(A) 8

(B) 10

(C) 12

(D) 14

20. A family budgeted $450 for groceries each month. In January, they spent $380. What percentage of the budget did they spend?

(A) 78.2 %

(B) 84.4 %

(C) 89.1 %

(D) 92.5 %

21. In a savings account, the interest rate is 3.5% annually. If $500 is deposited, how much interest will be earned after 2 years?

(A) $35

(B) $36.75

(C) $38.50

(D) $40.25

22. If a car travels at an average speed of 60 miles per hour, how far can it travel in 3.5 hours?

(A) 190 miles

(B) 205 miles

(C) 210 miles

(D) 215 miles

23. Which point on the number line best represents 1.35?

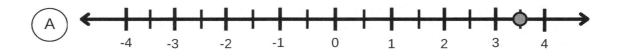

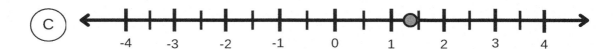

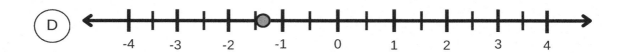

24. Javier bought 9 pounds of ground beef. He saved $8.37 by using a store coupon. How much did he save per pound of ground beef?

(A) $0.89

(B) $0.93

(C) $1.08

(D) $75.33

25. Elizabeth can type 28 words per minute. At this rate, how many words can Elizbeth type in 5.5 minutes?

(A) 154

(B) 157

(C) 159

(D) 162

26. Which situation could be described by the expression? $c + 2\frac{1}{2}$?

(A) Lila jogged c miles yesterday and $2\frac{1}{2}$ miles farther today

(B) Lila jogged c miles yesterday and $2\frac{1}{2}$ miles fewer today

(C) Lila jogged $2\frac{1}{2}$ miles yesterday and c miles fewer today

(D) Lila jogged $2\frac{1}{2}$ miles yesterday and c times as far today

27. The table below shows the average number of lunches bought in a cafeteria each day over a period of years.

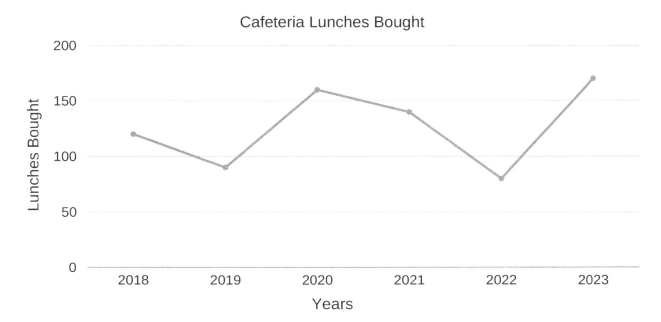

Cafeteria Lunches Bought

The greatest decrease in the number of lunches bought occurred between which two years?

(A) from 2019 to 2020

(B) from 2020 to 2021

(C) from 2021 to 2022

(D) from 2022 to 2023

28. A group of people went fishing for four days. Together, they caught 20 pounds of fish each day.

Day 1

Fish	Part of Total Pounds
Tuna	$\frac{5}{20}$
Snapper	$\frac{3}{20}$
Flounder	$\frac{8}{20}$
Mackerel	$\frac{4}{20}$

Day 2

Fish	Part of Total Pounds
Tuna	$\frac{10}{20}$
Snapper	$\frac{1}{20}$
Flounder	$\frac{4}{20}$
Mackerel	$\frac{5}{20}$

Day 3

Fish	Part of Total Pounds
Tuna	$\frac{6}{20}$
Snapper	$\frac{6}{20}$
Flounder	$\frac{5}{20}$
Mackerel	$\frac{3}{20}$

Day 4

Fish	Part of Total Pounds
Tuna	$\frac{4}{20}$
Snapper	$\frac{5}{20}$
Flounder	$\frac{3}{20}$
Mackerel	$\frac{8}{20}$

On which day was tuna 50% of the total catch?

(A) Day 1

(B) Day 2

(C) Day 3

(D) Day 4

29. Andrew constructed a triangle so that ∡1 and ∡2 and were the same size and ∡3 measured 80°.

What is the measure of ∡1?

A) 50°

B) 60°

C) 70°

D) 80°

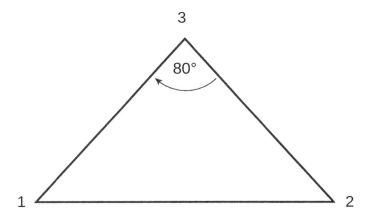

30. What is the volume, in cubic inches, of the school locker below?

A) 2880

B) 2580

C) 3900

D) 3600

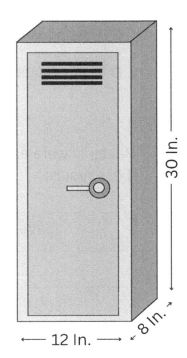

31. The trapezoid below can be divided into 3 identical triangles.

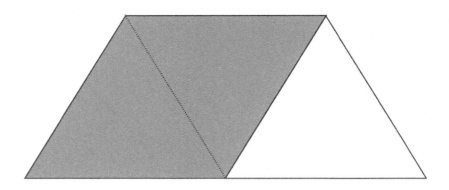

If the area of the shaded parallelogram is 16 square inches, what is the area of the trapezoid?

- (A) 8 square inches
- (B) 24 square inches
- (C) 32 square inches
- (D) 48 square inches

32. Students were asked how they traveled to school each day. The table below shows these results.

Type of Travel	Percentage
Bus	15%
Car	60%
Walk	20%
Bike	5%

Which graphic correctly displays this data?

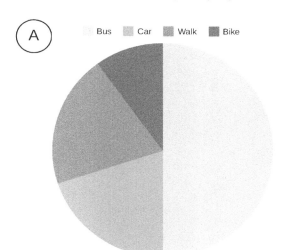

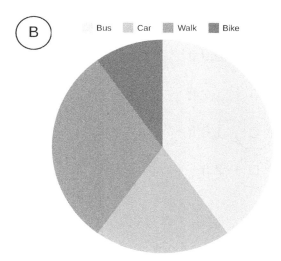

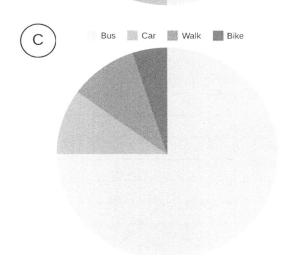

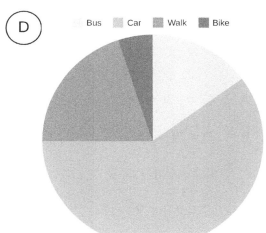

33. Simplify the expression: $(1\frac{7}{12} - \frac{3}{8}) + (2\frac{1}{3} - \frac{1}{4})$

- (A) $\frac{7}{20}$
- (B) $\frac{7}{24}$
- (C) $\frac{1}{9}$
- (D) $\frac{79}{24}$

34. A square patio has a perimeter of 3.6 ft. What is the lengths of one side?

(A) 0.9 ft

(B) 1.2 ft

(C) 1.6 ft

(D) 2 ft

35. Mia reads a book at a steady pace. Mia graphs her progress through the book by putting the time in hours t on the horizontal axis and chapters remaining C on the vertical axis. Which equation describes Mia's graph?

(A) $C = -3t + 24$

(B) $C = 3t - 24$

(C) $C = -24t + 3$

(D) $C = 24t + 3$

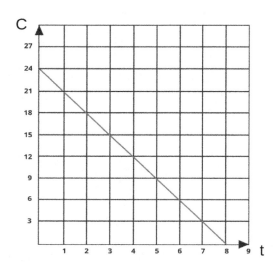

36. Which set of number are ordered from greatest to least?

(A) 4.220; 4.200; 4.301; 4.400

(B) 2.110; 2.120; 2.130; 2.160

(C) 4.000; 3.900; 3.810; 3.800

(D) 3.350; 3.542; 3.535; 3.530

37. The map below shows the locations of rides at an amusement park. Maria was at the point (−1, −4). She walked 2 units west and 2 units north. Which ride did she walk to?

(A) Giant Coaster

(B) Little Dipper

(C) Sky Train

(D) Ferris Wheel

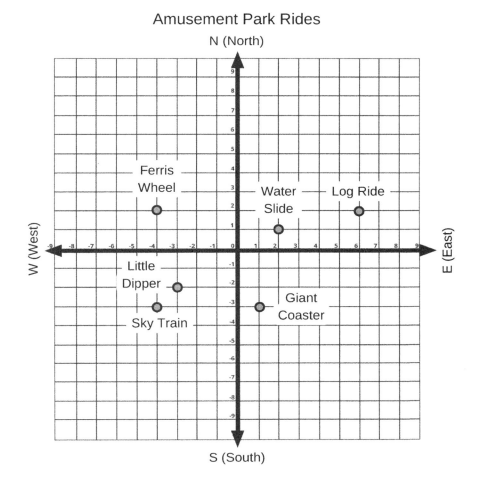

Amusement Park Rides

38. What is the value of p that makes this equation true?
44 · 73 = 44 (p + 3)

(A) 41

(B) 47

(C) 70

(D) 73

91

39. Bill played a game and scored 5 times. If each time Bill scored he earned p points, which expression represents the total number of points that Bill earned?

(A) $p + 5$

(B) $p - 5$

(C) $p \cdot 5$

(D) $p : 5$

40. The table below shows the distances traveled by four runners during a race

Runner	Distance Travelled (Miles)
A	3.72
B	4.05
C	3.98
D	3.50

Which statement is true?

(A) The distance traveled by Runner C is less than the distance traveled by Runner D.

(B) The distance traveled by Runner A is greater than the distance traveled by Runner B.

(C) The distance traveled by Runner B is less than the distance traveled by Runner D.

(D) The distance traveled by Runner C is greater than the distance traveled by Runner A.

41. A rectangular prism container measures 4.5 ft in length, 6.5 ft in width, and 10.4 ft in height. How many liters of water can the container hold?

- (A) 6,614.589 liters
- (B) 8,614.944 liters
- (C) 10,005.3 liters
- (D) 12,059.972 liters

42. John earns a monthly allowance of $50. He decides to save 20% of his allowance each month and spend the rest. How much money will John save from his allowance each month?

- (A) $10
- (B) $15
- (C) $20
- (D) $25

43. A group of 5 friends went out for dinner. The bill total came to $85.75, including tax and tip. If they decide to split the bill equally among them, how much money, in dollars and cents, did each person pay?

- (A) $17.75
- (B) $17.15
- (C) $17.25
- (D) $17.50

44. A recipe for chocolate chip cookies is enough for 12 cookies and require the following ingredients:

1 Cup Flour

$\frac{1}{4}$ Teaspoon Baking Soda

$\frac{1}{4}$ Teaspoon Salt

$\frac{1}{2}$ Cup Unsalted Butter

$\frac{1}{2}$ Cup Granulated Sugar

1 Large Egg

$\frac{1}{2}$ Teaspoon Vanilla Extract

$\frac{3}{4}$ Cup Semisweet Chocolate Chips

If Emily wants to make 30 cookies instead of 12, how many ingredients does she need to add? Show your work.

45. Olivia works as a tutor. She charges $20 per hour for one-on-one tutoring sessions and $30 per hour for group tutoring sessions. Last week, Olivia conducted the following tutoring sessions:

- On Monday, she tutored 3 students individually for 2 hours each.

- On Tuesday, she tutored a group of 5 students for 1.5 hours.

- On Wednesday, she tutored 2 students individually for 3 hours each.

- On Thursday, she tutored a group of 4 students for 2 hours.

Olivia used the following expression to determine the amount of money she earned from tutoring last week:

20 (3 · 2) + 30 (5 · 1.5) + 20 (2 · 3) + 30 (4 · 2)

How much money did Olivia earn from tutoring last week?

A $490

B $550

C $640

D $705

46. Susan has 324 boxes, and each box has a volume of 1 cubic inch. She wants to use them to construct a rectangular prism with dimensions as follows: 15 inches in length, 8 inches in width, and 3 inches in height. Does Susan have enough boxes to construct the prism?

A Yes, Susan has enough boxes.

B No, Susan does not have enough boxes.

C Susan has exactly enough boxes.

D I don't know.

47. Simplify the expression: (7.5 · 2.8 - 4.75) · 1.6 + 2.08 · 0.5

A 15.69

B 16.78

C 21.62

D 27.04

48. Simplify the expression: $0.75 \cdot 1\frac{2}{3} - (\frac{4}{5} + \frac{1}{2}) : 3\frac{1}{4} + \frac{3}{4}$

(A) 55

(B) $\frac{3}{5}$

(C) 76.5

(D) $1\frac{3}{5}$

49. Susan bought a soccer ball on sale for $25, which was $\frac{1}{5}$ off the original price. What decimal represents the discount she received?

(A) 0.05

(B) 0.15

(C) 0.20

(D) 0.50

50. Which of these is correct:

(A) $50\% < \frac{3}{4} < 0.74$

(B) $\frac{3}{4} > 50\% > 0.74$

(C) $0.74 > 50\% > \frac{3}{4}$

(D) $50\% < 0.74 < \frac{3}{4}$

Answers Practice Test 4

1.B, 9.3 in

2.D,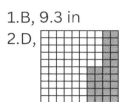

3.D, (9, 2)

4.B, $0.40

5.B, $\frac{1}{13}$

6.A,

Hours Worked	1	2	3	4	5
Money Earned	$6	$12	$18	$24	$30

7.B, 30 minutes to 35 minutes

8.B and E,

Since $\frac{5}{15}$ is less than $\frac{2}{5}$, the total of $\frac{5}{15}$ is not reasonable

The fractions $\frac{3}{10}$ and $\frac{2}{5}$ are each greater than $\frac{1}{4}$ so the total must be greater than $\frac{1}{2}$. The fraction $\frac{5}{15}$ is less than $\frac{1}{2}$, so the total of $\frac{5}{15}$ is not reasonable.

9.C, 30

10.C, $3\frac{17}{18}$

11.D, 0.60

12.C, 37.5%

13.a=9, b=5

14.A, 31.04

15.B, $\frac{19}{90}$

16.C, 37

17.A, -3

18.B, 421.824 square inches

19.C, 12

20.B, 84.4%

21.A, $35

22.C, 210 miles

23.C, 1.35

24.B, $0.93

25.A, 154

26.A, Lila jogged c miles yesterday and 2 (1/2) miles farther today

27.C, from 2021 to 2022

28.B, Day 2

29.A, 50°

30.A, 288 cubic inches

31.B, 24 square inches

32.D,

33.D, $\frac{79}{24}$

34.A, 0.9 ft

35.A, C=−3t+24

36.C, 4.000; 3.900; 3.810; 3.800

37.B, Little Dipper

38.C, 70

39.C, p · 5

40.D, The distance traveled by Runner C is greater than the distance traveled by Runner A.

41.B, 8,614.944 liters

42.A, $10

43.B, $17.15

44.Emily needs to add 1.5 cups of flour, 3/8 teaspoons of baking soda, 3/8 teaspoons of salt, 0.75 cups of unsalted butter, 0.75 cups of granulated sugar, one and a half eggs, 0.75 teaspoons of vanilla extract and 1.125 cups of semisweet chocolate chips.

45.D, $705

46.B, No, Susan does not have enough boxes.

47.D, 27.04

48.D, 8/5

49.C, 0.20

50.D, 50% < 0.74 < $\frac{3}{4}$

97

PRACTICE TEST 5

GET STARTED $\rightarrow$

1. What is the value of ẋ in the following equation? $\frac{2}{5} \cdot x + \frac{3}{10} = 1\frac{1}{2}$

- (A) 1
- (B) 2
- (C) 3
- (D) 4

2. A traveler traveled at the same speed from point A to point C via point B and covered 28 miles. He traveled for 3.5 hours from point A to point B and for $3\frac{1}{2}$ hours from B to C. At what speed was the traveler moving from point A to point C?

- (A) 8 miles per hour
- (B) 10 miles per hour
- (C) 50 miles per hour
- (D) 4 miles per hour

3. What value for m makes this equation true? $(8 \cdot 37) = (8 \cdot 30) + (8 \cdot m)$

- (A) 7
- (B) 10
- (C) 50
- (D) 75

4. John runs $\frac{8}{10}$ miles every day. How many miles does he run in 30 days?

(A) 18

(B) 24

(C) 30

(D) 38

5. Maria spent $1\frac{1}{3}$ hours reading and $\frac{3}{4}$ hour doing chores. How many total hours did Maria spend on these activities?

(A) $1\frac{1}{3}$

(B) $1\frac{4}{7}$

(C) $2\frac{1}{12}$

(D) $2\frac{1}{6}$

6. Which of the following sets of equivalent fractions, decimals and percent is incorrect?

(A) $0.39 = \frac{39}{100} = 39\%$

(B) $0.534 = \frac{534}{1000} = 53.4\%$

(C) $0.9 = \frac{90}{100} = 90\%$

(D) $6.07 = \frac{607}{1000} = 60.7\%$

7. Mrs. Smith noticed that $\frac{1}{4}$ of the class had completed the test within 30 minutes. What percent of the class was still working on the test?

- (A) 25%
- (B) 50%
- (C) 75%
- (D) 80%

8. A librarian arranged some books on the shelf using the Dewey decimal system. Choose the group of books numbers that is listed in order from greatest to least.

- (A) 726.3, 726.02, 726.101, 726.010
- (B) 726.02, 726.3, 726.101, 726.010
- (C) 726.3, 726.101, 726.02, 726.010
- (D) 726.010, 726.02, 726.101, 726.3

9. Four students are comparing their heights. Ted's height is $4\frac{1}{4}$ feet, Donald's height is 4.8 feet, Janson's height is $4\frac{1}{3}$ feet, and Justin's height is 4.2 feet. Which student is the shortest?

- (A) Ted
- (B) Donald
- (C) Jason
- (D) Justin

10. Arrange $\frac{1}{2}$, 5^1 , $\frac{3}{4}$, 0.85 , 80% and 2^2 from least to greatest.

(A) $\frac{1}{2}$, $\frac{3}{4}$, 2^2 , 5^1 , 80% , 0.85

(B) $\frac{3}{4}$, $\frac{1}{2}$, 80% , 0.85 , 5^1 , 2^2

(C) 80% , $\frac{1}{2}$, $\frac{3}{4}$, 2^2 , 5^1 , 0.85

(D) $\frac{1}{2}$, $\frac{3}{4}$, 80% , 0.85 , 2^2 , 5^1

11. Mrs. Patel is constructing a swimming pool in her backyard. The pool will have dimensions of 2.5 ft deep by 5.4 ft wide by 10 ft long. If the cost of concrete is $6 per cubic ft, how much will Mrs. Patel need to pay for the concrete for her pool?

(A) 726

(B) 826

(C) 810

(D) 710

12. What is the volume of this figure (assuming that each cube has 1 cubic unit of volume)?

(A) 12 cubic units

(B) 16 cubic units

(C) 28 cubic units

(D) 40 cubic units

100

13. Suzan collected 560 cups of rainwater on Saturday. She collected 3.5 pints of rainwater on Sunday. How many total cups of rainwater did Suzan collect on Saturday and Sunday?

- (A) 400
- (B) 567
- (C) 891
- (D) 9100

14. A rectangular container has a square base with an area of 25 square inches. The container has a height of 4 inches. What is the volume, in cubic inches, of the container? Show your work.

15. Simplify the expression 64 : (15 - 5 + 12 : 2) + 9 · 2 - 1

- (A) 18
- (B) 21
- (C) 30
- (D) 44

16. The line plot shows the distance, in miles, that Jenny walked on 5 different days.

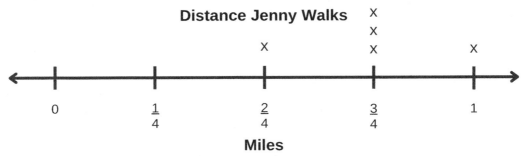

Distance Jenny Walks

Miles

What is the total distance Jenny walked, in miles? Show your work.

17. The partial school schedule above shows the start times and end times of class periods. Except for lunch, all classes are the same length.

Middle School Bell Schedule		
Class Period	Start Time	End Time
Second	8:40 AM	9:36 AM
Third	9:40 AM	10:36 AM
Fourth	10:40 AM	11:36 AM
Lunch	11:40 AM	12:15 PM
Fifth		1:15 PM

What is the missing start time for fifth period?

A) 12:15 PM

B) 12:19 PM

C) 12:40 PM

D) 12:50 PM

18. Kerri ran the same distance in four different races. Her times were 18.04 seconds, 21.39 seconds, 12.99 seconds, and 14.14 seconds. If the individual times are rounded to the nearest one-tenth of a second, what is the estimate of Kerri's total time for all four races?

(A) 66.6 Seconds

(B) 66.5 Seconds

(C) 66 Seconds

(D) 65.5 Seconds

19. Tom is driving at a speed of 50 miles per hour. At 2:00 he sees the following sign:

Applebee	11 Miles
Beauville	41 Miles
Caanan	62 Miles
Denton	98 Miles

Tom continues at the same speed. At 2:30 how far from Caanan will he be?

(A) 12 Miles

(B) 25 Miles

(C) 37 Miles

(D) 43 Miles

20. A Manufacturing Company packages a product for shipping by wrapping tape around the package as shown in the diagram (assume that there's tape on the opposite sides of the package as well). An additional 10% length of tape per package is needed for overlap. What is the total length of tape needed per package?

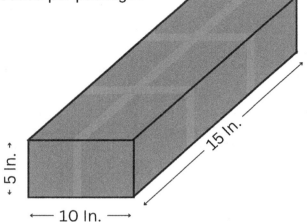

- (A) 25 inches
- (B) 150 inches
- (C) 110 inches
- (D) 55 inches

5 In.

15 In.

10 In.

21. At the beginning of a class period, half of the students in a class go to the library. Later in the period, half of the remaining students go to the computer lab. If there are 8 students remaining in the class, how many students were originally in the class?

- (A) 20 Students
- (B) 28 Students
- (C) 32 Students
- (D) 40 Students

22. A glass tabletop is supported by a rectangular pedestal. If the tabletop is 8 inches wider than the pedestal on each side, what is the perimeter of the glass tabletop?

- (A) 198 Inches
- (B) 232 Inches
- (C) 322 Inches
- (D) 450 Inches

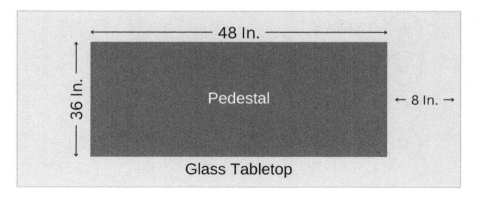

48 In.

36 In.

Pedestal

← 8 In. →

Glass Tabletop

23. The map below shows the location of 4 different stores.

Which store is at the point (3,-1)

A Hardware Store

B Grocery Store

C Shoe Store

D Toy Store

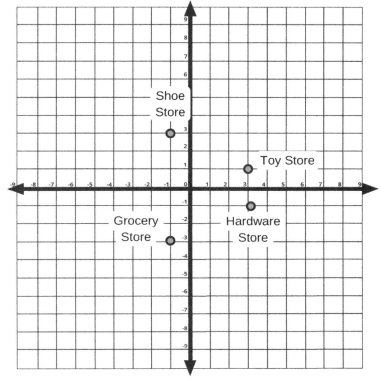

24. Line *m* is represented by the equation y = 4.

Which ordered pair is located on line *m*

A (1,4)

B (0,0)

C (4,1)

D (4,0)

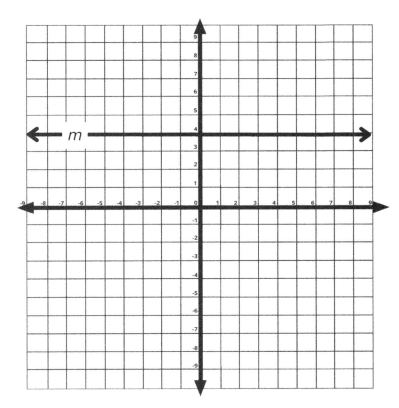

105

25. Which table represents values of x and y such that y = x + 5?

A

x	y
-1	4
0	5

B

x	y
-1	-6
0	-5

C

x	y
2	5
5	0

D

x	y
2	3
3	0

26. Triangle A and B are congruent.

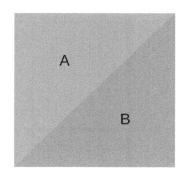 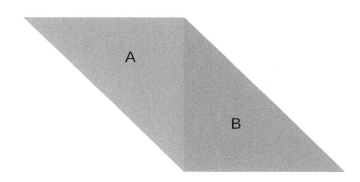

If the area of the rectangle is 7 square units, what is the area, in square units, of the parallelogram?

A) 3.5

B) 7

C) 14

D) 18.5

27. Simona's piano teacher kept this record of Simona's progress in a song she is memorizing. The x-axis represents the days that have passed, and the y-axis represents the percentage of the song that she has memorized.

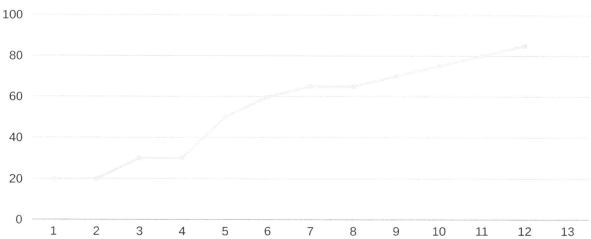

How many days of practice did it take for Simona to memorize half of the song?

A) 4

B) 5

C) 6

D) 8

28. Based on the graph above, what is the average percentage of the song memorized during the represented practice days?

A) 40.5%

B) 49.23%

C) 54.17%

D) 68.89%

29. Terry charges $4.00 per hour to baby-sit. What equation could Terry use to find the number of hours (h) he needs to baby-site in order to earn $50.00?

A 4 + h - 50

B $\frac{h}{4}$ - 50

C h - 4 - 50

D 4h = 50

30. Which equation could have been used to create the function table?

A $y = \frac{x}{2}$

B $y = 2x$

C $y = x - 4$

D $y = x + 4$

x	y
-9	-5
-2	2
4	8
11	15

31. Tina goes to the grocery store to buy each of the items on her list. Tina rounds the cost of each item to the nearest dollar. What is the estimated total cost of these items?

A $15.00

B $16.00

C $17.00

D $18.00

Toothpaste	$3.99
Bread	$2.45
Milk	$2.69
Apples	$3.10
Cereal	$4.89

108

32. A bar graph is given.

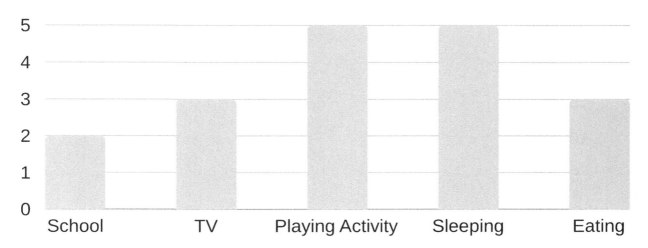

Which circle graph could represent the information in the bar graph?

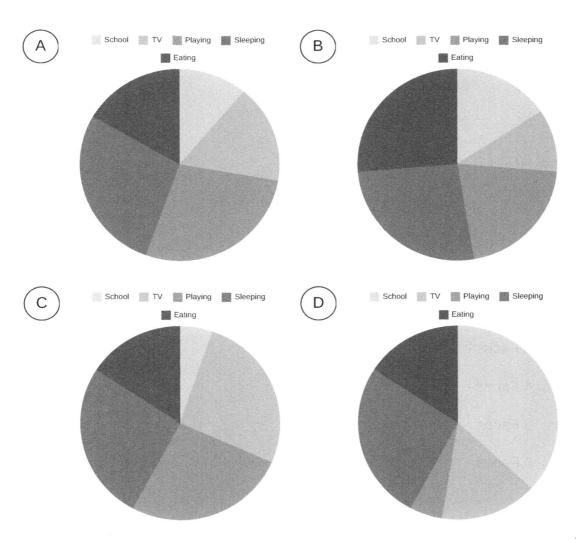

33. A teacher asked the fifth graders about their favorite activities.

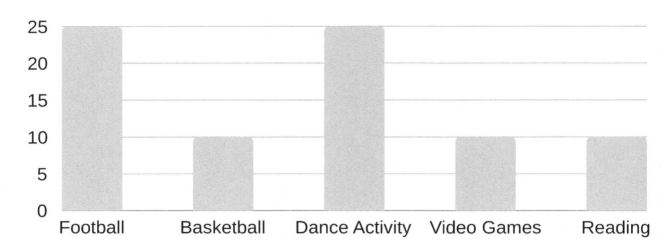

What is the total number of fifth graders represented on the graph?

(A) 10

(B) 25

(C) 65

(D) 80

34. How many faces does the prism have?

(A) 3 Faces

(B) 4 Faces

(C) 5 Faces

(D) 6 Faces

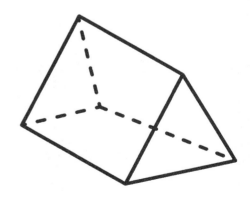

35. Simplify the expression $(\frac{1}{2} + 1.2 : 0.25 - 2.3) : 7\frac{1}{2}$

(A) 0.25

(B) 0.4

(C) 0.66

(D) 0.98

36. During the first month, Alex saved \$x each week for n weeks. During the second month, he increased his savings to \$y each week for the same n weeks. Which equation can be used to find m, the total amount of money Alex saved during these two months?

(A) $m = x \cdot y \cdot n$

(B) $m = (x + y) \cdot n$

(C) $m = x : y - n$

(D) $m = x + y + n$

37. A bakery sells boxes of assorted chocolates for \$12 each. The total revenue from selling these boxes is \$540. How many boxes of chocolates were sold?

(A) 42

(B) 45

(C) 48

(D) 50

38. In the hundred grid below, shade the squares to represent 45% of the total area.

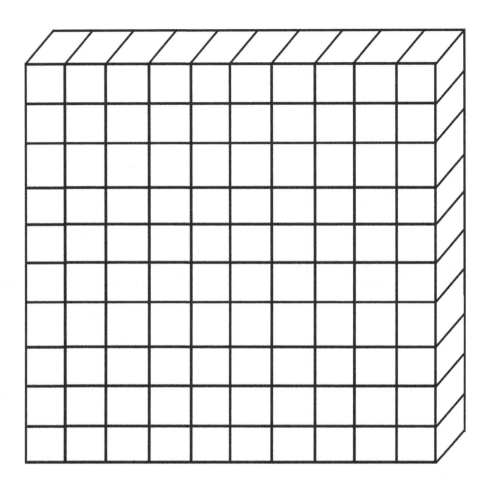

39. A vending machine contains 200 snacks. There are 40 bags of chips and 60 candy bars. The rest of the snacks are granola bars. Which equation can be used to find g, the total number of granola bars in the vending machine?

    Ⓐ g = 200 + 60 − 40

    Ⓑ g = 200 − 60 + 40

    Ⓒ g = 200 − 60 − 40

    Ⓓ g = 200 + 60 + 40

40. Jennifer wants to make lemonade for a party. She decides to adjust the recipe to make 5 times the original amount of lemonade. If the original recipe requires:

- 2 cups of lemon juice
- $1\frac{1}{2}$ cups of granulated sugar
- 6 cups of water
- Ice cubes

How many cups of granulated sugar will Jennifer need for the adjusted recipe?

A) 6 Cups

B) 7.5 Cups

C) 10 Cups

D) 15.5 Cups

41. A worker can finish a certain task in 9 days, while another worker can finish the same task in 12 days. If a third worker joins them, the three of them can finish the task together in 4 days. In how many days can the third worker finish the same task alone?

A) 13 Days

B) 15 Days

C) 18 Days

D) 20 Days

42. From two places, two cars started simultaneously towards each other. The first would have covered the distance in 12 hours, and the second in 20 hours. After how many hours from the start will the cars meet?

(A) 6 Hours

(B) 7.5 Hours

(C) 9.5 Hours

(D) 10 Hours

43. Mr. Ben is constructing a rectangular prism-shaped storage shed in his backyard. If the shed has a length of 12 feet, a width of 8.5 feet, and a height of 6 feet, what is the volume of space the shed can hold?

(A) 512 Cubic Feet

(B) 612 Cubic Feet

(C) 712 Cubic Feet

(D) 900 Cubic Feet

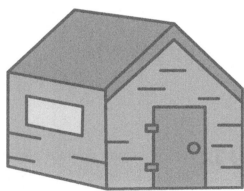

44. Mr. Johnson has 205 identical rectangular wooden shelves, each measuring 32 in long and 8 in wide. He wants to make 12 wooden boxes (as shown in the picture on the left). Does Mr. Johnson have enough shelves to construct these wooden boxes? (The bottom of the wooden boxes is made of five identical long wooden shelves used as sides.)

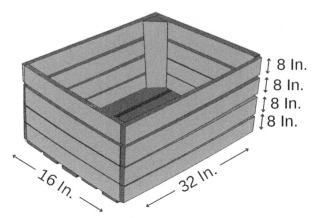

8 In.
8 In.
8 In.
8 In.
16 In.
32 In.

(A) Yes, Mr. Johnson has enough shelves to construct the wooden boxes.

(B) No, Mr. Johnson does not have enough shelves to construct the wooden boxes.

(C) We cannot determine based on the information provided

45. In Tim's house, a rectangular swimming pool (blue) whose length 30 ft and width 20 ft is surrounded by grass (green). The pool with the grassy area make a large rectangle whose length is 50 ft and width 40 ft. What area is occupied by the grass?

(A) 550 Square Ft

(B) 800 Square Ft

(C) 1400 Square Ft

(D) 2300 Square Ft

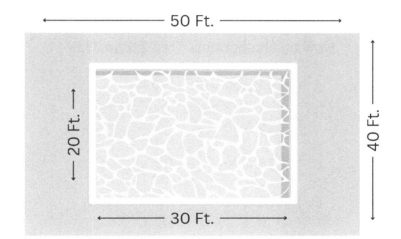

46. Two hiking trails have the same start point and end point.

- Trail 1 presses through rest area A
- Trail 2 passes through rest area B and rest area C

The map shows the distances along the two trails in miles.

Map of Distances Along Two Hiking Trails

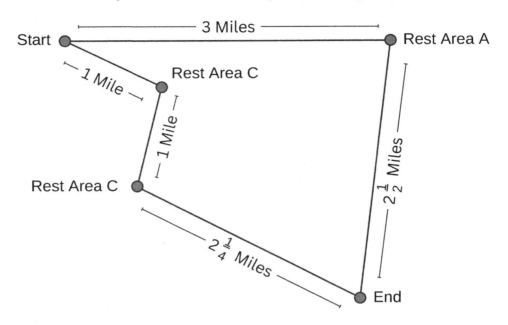

How much shorter is Trail 2 than Trail 1?

- (A) 0.75 Mile
- (B) 1.25 Mile
- (C) 1.75 Mile
- (D) 2.25 Mile

47. Three toy cars and 4 toy trains cost $18. Two toy cars and 3 toy trains cost $13. What is the price of one toy car and the price of one toy train if both prices are whole numbers of Dollars?

- (A) Price of 1 car is $2 and the price of a train is $3
- (B) Price of 1 car is $3 and the price of a train is $1
- (C) Price of 1 car is $4 and the price of a train is $5
- (D) Price of 1 car is $2.5 and the price of a train is $4.1

48. It takes John 25 minutes to walk to the car park and 45 to drive to work. At what time should he get out of the house in order to get to work at 9:00 a.m.?

- (A) 6:00
- (B) 7:00
- (C) 7:50
- (D) 8:10

49. A factory produced 2300 TV sets in its first year of production. 4500 sets were produced in its second year and 500 more sets were produced in its third year than in its second year. How many TV sets were produced in three years?

- (A) 11,800
- (B) 12,000
- (C) 14,500
- (D) 18,300

50. Kim can walk 4 miles in one hour. How long does it take Kim to walk 18 miles?

- (A) 3h 30 min
- (B) 4h 30 min
- (C) 5h 30 min
- (D) 6h 30 min

Answers Practice Test 5

1. C, 3
2. D, 4 miles per hour
3. A, 7 miles per hour
4. B, 24
5. C, $2\frac{1}{12}$
6. D, $6.07 = \frac{607}{1000} = 60.7\%$
7. C, 75%
8. C, 726.3, 726.101, 726.02, 726.010
9. D, Justin
10. D, $\frac{1}{2}$, $\frac{3}{4}$, 80% , 0.85 , 2^2 , 5^1
11. C, 810$
12. C, 28 cubic units
13. B, 567
14. 100 cubic in
15. B, 21
16. 3.75 miles
17. B, 12:19 P.M
18. B, 66.5 seconds
19. C, 37 Miles
20. C, 110 inches
21. C, 32
22. B, 232 inches
23. A, (3, −1)
24. A, (1,4)
25. A
26. B, 7
27. B, 5
28. C, 54.17%
29. D, 4h = 50
30. D, y = x + 4
31. C, $17.00
32. A,

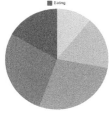

33. D, 80
34. C, 5 faces
35. B, 0.4
36. B, m = (x + y) · n
37. B, 45
38.

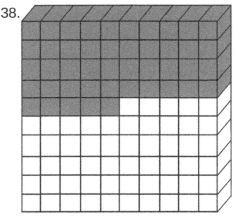

39. C, g = 200 − 60 − 40
40. B, 7.5 Cups
41. C, 18 days
42. B, 7.5 hours
43. B, 612 cubic feet
44. A, Yes, Mr. Johnson has enough shelves to construct the wooden boxes.
45. C, 1400 square ft
46. B, 1.25 miles
47. A, Price of 1 car is $2 and the price of a train is $3
48. C, 7:50
49. A, 11,800
50. B, 4h 30 min

ARE YOU OR YOUR CHILD FINDING CERTAIN MATH PROBLEMS CHALLENGING?

Scan the QR-code below to access the complete step-by-step solutions for this book. It's designed to make learning math simpler and boost your child's confidence.

STEP-BY-STEP SOLUTIONS

FOR EACH EXERCISE IN THIS BOOK.

STAAR

STATE OF TEXAS ASSESSMENTS OF ACADEMIC READINESS

GRADE 5
SCIENCE

Jason Reed

First Edition

Table of Contents

Introduction

About the STAAR Science Tests

The 5th-grade Science STAAR test includes a total of 42 questions. Among these, there are multiple-choice questions where students must choose the correct answer from the provided options. The remaining questions are open-ended, requiring students to express their thoughts and provide explanations.

About the Science STAAR Full-Length Tests in This Book

The practice questions included in this book are designed to replicate the Science STAAR tests accurately. They provide your child with a valuable opportunity to understand key concepts and familiarize themselves with the format, types of questions, and time constraints they will encounter on the STAAR test.

The tests target all required categories, ensuring your child masters Matter and Energy, Force, Motion, and Energy, Earth and Space, and Organisms and Environments.

Repetition is a proven method for effective studying. We firmly believe in the power of practice, which is why we've included multiple practice questions for each STAAR category in this book.

By working through these practice tests, your child can:

- **Improve time management:** They will become adept at managing their time efficiently during the test, ensuring they complete all sections within the allocated time.

- **Build confidence:** Repeatedly solving problems in a format similar to the actual test will boost their confidence, reducing anxiety on test day.

- **Identify weaknesses:** These questions will help pinpoint and target specific areas where your child may need additional review and practice.

- **Enhance problem-solving skills:** Regular practice hones problem-solving skills and strategies, enabling your child to tackle challenging questions effectively.

- **Score higher:** Through focused practice and familiarization with the test structure, your child can strive for higher scores on the STAAR test.

The questions in this book closely mirror those found in the actual STAAR tests, ensuring that your child gains a deep understanding of the test's structure and content. By working through these practice questions, they will be well-equipped to achieve success on the Science STAAR test.

As parents, educators, or instructors, your support and encouragement play a pivotal role in your child's academic journey. We encourage you to actively engage with your child's science education, using these resources as tools to enhance their learning experience.

Dear Parents,

Thank you for purchasing the STAAR Science Practice Workbook for grade 5.

As an independent author, I have put a great deal of effort into ensuring the quality and accuracy of the content provided. Each problem has been carefully solved and reviewed to provide the best learning experience.

However, despite the rigorous efforts to maintain high standards, occasional mistakes can occur. If you come across any errors or discrepancies in the book or the solutions, please do not hesitate to reach out. Your feedback is invaluable in helping to improve the quality of this workbook.

For any corrections, questions, or comments, please contact me at *jasonreedbooks@gmail.com*. Your assistance in identifying and rectifying any issues is greatly appreciated.

Thank you for your understanding and support.

Sincerely,

Jason Reed

PRACTICE TEST 1

GET STARTED →

1. The Earth moves around the Sun while continuously rotating on its axis. How much time does it take for the Earth to complete one full orbit around the Sun?

A 24 hours

B 30 days

C 6 months

D 1 year

2. Which planet in our solar system is closest to the Sun?

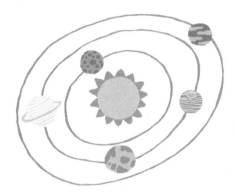

A Mercury

B Venus

C Earth

D Mars

3. What causes the phenomenon of day and night on Earth?

A The Earth's orbit around the Sun.

B The Earth's rotation on its axis.

C The tilt of the Earth's axis.

D The Earth's gravitational pull.

4. What is a food chain?

(A) A type of plant structure in charge of nutrient and water distribution.

(B) A chain used to catch food by different insect and arachnid species.

(C) A series of organisms each dependent on the next as a source of food.

(D) A sequence of weather events that influence the availability of food.

5. Which of the following food chains correctly shows the flow of energy in a marine ecosystem?

(A) Plankton → fish → seals → sharks

(B) Seals → sharks → fish → plankton

(C) Fish → sharks → seals → plankton

(D) Plankton → seals → sharks → fish

6. In a freshwater lake ecosystem, what is the primary source of energy?

(A) Phytoplankton

(B) Fish

(C) Birds

(D) Algae

7. How can we reduce our carbon footprint?

- (A) By driving around your city to visit new restaurants.
- (B) By taking note of all the types of waste you produce.
- (C) By travelling to natural protected areas by airplane.
- (D) By using public transport and reducing energy consumption.

8. Which inference can be made by comparing these diagrams?

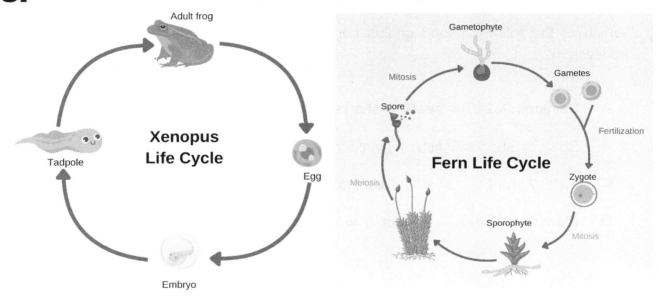

- (A) Plants require more kinetic energy than animals to undergo changes from a young organism to a mature organism.

- (B) Both animals and plants undergo a series of changes throughout their life cycle that enable them to survive and reproduce.

- (C) Animals are more likely than plants to adapt to changes in the environment for survival.

- (D) Animals and plants mutually depend on each other for survival.

9. A student observes the water cycle in the following image.

The Water Cycle

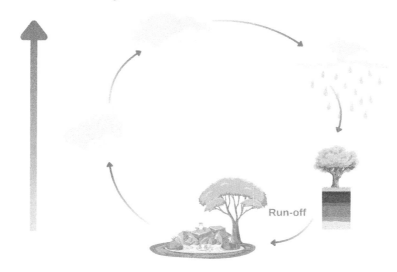

Run-off

Which energy is involved in the evaporation of water from lake to clouds?

(A) Electrical energy

(B) Chemical energy

(C) Thermal energy

(D) Gravitational energy

10. A student places a piece of iron in a fire. What causes the iron to become red-hot?

(A) The iron absorbs heat from the fire.

(B) The iron reflects heat from the fire.

(C) The iron passes through the heat from the fire.

(D) The iron emits heat to the fire.

11. This question has two parts. Answer Part A with the help of the following image. Then, answer Part B.

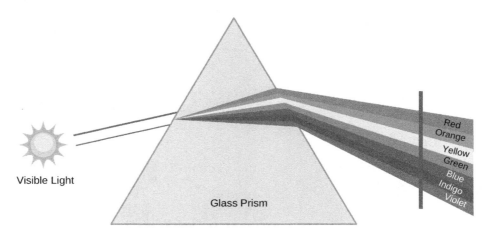

Visible Light

Glass Prism

Red
Orange
Yellow
Green
Blue
Indigo
Violet

Part A

A student shines a beam of white light through a prism, and the light spreads out into a spectrum of colors. Which statement BEST describes what happens to the light as it passes through the prism?

(A) The light is absorbed by the prism.

(B) The light is reflected by the prism.

(C) The light is refracted by the prism.

(D) The light is diffused by the prism.

Part B

Which statement BEST explains the answer to Part A?

(A) The prism absorbs different wavelengths of light at different rates.

(B) The prism reflects different wavelengths of light at different angles.

(C) The prism bends (refracts) different wavelengths of light in different amounts.

(D) The prism diffuses the light, scattering it in all directions.

12. A soccer ball is kicked across a field. What force causes the ball to eventually stop rolling?

A Air resistance pushing against the ball.

B Gravity pulling the ball downward.

C Friction between the ball and the grass.

D Elastic force from the impact of the kick.

13. Students observe the picture below where particles of an unknown material are added to pure water. After mixing, the particles sediment to the bottom of the container.

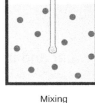

Pure water   Mixing   Sedimentation

Which conclusion can be made from image?

A The particles have a higher density than water.

B The particles have a lower density than water.

C The particles have the same density as water.

D The particles dissolve completely in water.

14. A laser pointer is directed at a mirror on a wall. The beam reflects off the mirror and hits another wall. What property of light does this demonstration show?

A Light absorption

B Light reflection

C Light diffusion

D Light refraction

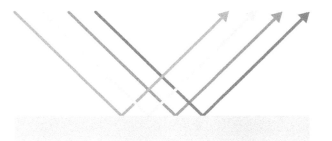

10

15. What process causes dew to form on grass in the morning?

(A) Water vapor melted on the grass.

(B) Water vapor evaporated off the grass.

(C) Water vapor condensed on the grass .

(D) Water vapor froze on the grass.

16. A student has a mixture of iron nails, marbles, and sand. How can the student separate the nails from the mixture?

(A) Dissolve the mixture in water and then filter it.

(B) Use a magnet to attract the nails.

(C) Pour the mixture through filter paper.

(D) Heat the mixture to melt the iron nails.

17. In a kitchen experiment, a student mixes cooking oil and vinegar. How can the student separate the oil from the vinegar?

(A) Heat the mixture until the oil evaporates.

(B) Use a magnet to attract the oil droplets.

(C) Pour the mixture through filter paper.

(D) Place the mixture in a refrigerator to solidify the oil.

18. A table of the properties of four different samples of matter is shown.

Sample	Conducts Electricity	Conducts Heat	Soluble in Water	Physical State at Room Temperature
1	No	No	No	Solid
2	Yes	Yes	No	Solid
3	No	Yes	Yes	Liquid
4	Yes	Yes	No	Liquid

Which answer is correct for sample 1?

A Sample 1 is plastic.

B Sample 1 is iron.

C Sample 1 is alcohol.

D Sample 1 is oxygen.

19. Students made a chart classifying animal behaviors.

Inherited	Learned
Turtle nesting on a beach	Bee building a hive
Chick imprinting on its mother	Dolphin learning tricks in captivity
Caterpillar spinning a coccon	Monkey washing food before eating

Which animal behavior is NOT correctly classified?

A Turtle nesting on a beach.

B Chick imprinting on its mother.

C Caterpillar spinning a cocoon.

D Bee building a hive.

12

20. Volcanoes and calderas are two geological features found in volcanic regions. Which statement best describes how volcanoes and calderas are similar?

- (A) Both are formed by underground magma chambers.
- (B) Both are created by erosion and weathering.
- (C) Both are part of tectonic plate boundaries.
- (D) Both are shaped by meteorite impacts.

21. This question has two parts. First, answer Part A. Then, answer Part B.

Part A

A student places an ice cube on a plate and leaves it at room temperature. Which statement BEST describes what will happen to the ice cube over time?

- (A) The ice cube will increase in size.
- (B) The ice cube will decrease in size.
- (C) The ice cube will remain the same size.
- (D) The ice cube will become warmer but remain solid.

Part B

Which statement BEST explains the answer to Part A?

- (A) The ice cube absorbs heat from the surroundings, causing it to melt.
- (B) The ice cube absorbs cold from the surroundings, causing it to grow.
- (C) The ice cube releases cold to the surroundings, causing it to stay solid.
- (D) The ice cube releases heat to the surroundings, causing it to remain the same size.

22. A student mixed salt into a glass of water and stirred it. After a few minutes, the salt particles were no longer visible, and the water tasted salty. What most likely happened to the salt?

A   The salt evaporated into the air.

B   The salt dissolved in the water.

C   The salt sank to the bottom of the glass.

D   The salt reacted with the water to form a new substance.

23. Which statement describes an animal interacting with a non-living part of the environment?

A   A fish swims through water.

B   A bird builds a nest in a tree.

C   A cat chases a mouse.

D   A cow eats grass.

24. A student drew the following pictures to show the day-night cycle of Earth.

Based on the pictures, how many hours of the nighttime is in a day-night cycle?

A   9 hours

B   10 hours

C   11 hours

D   24 hours

Sunrise: 7:15 AM
Sunset: 8:15 PM

25. Maple trees grow to be 10 to 45 meters tall. Their wide branches are covered with broad leaves, and their roots penetrate deeply into the soil. Maple trees drop their leaves in autumn.

Characteristics of Four Ecosystems

Ecosystem	Temperature	Yearly Precipitation	Soil
1	Cold winters and warm summers	Between 70 and 150 cm of rain	Moist, fertile soil
2	Warm year-round	Less than 40 cm of rain	Dry, sandy soil
3	Hot summers and mild winters	Between 60 and 100 cm of rain	Rocky, thin soil
4	Cool-to-cold winters and warm summers	More than 200 cm of rain	Well-drained, rich soil

In which ecosystem would forests of maple trees be most likely to survive?

A) Ecosystem 1

B) Ecosystem 2

C) Ecosystem 3

D) Ecosystem 4

26. A three-step process is shown: **Melting → Cooling → Crystallization**

Which of these are most likely formed by the process shown?

A) Glaciers

B) Igneous rocks

C) Fossil fuels

D) Sand dunes

27. Which material is known for being lightweight yet strong, and often used in airplane construction?

A) Iron

B) Aluminum

C) Copper

D) Lead

28. Which environmental impact is the most likely to occur when constructing a new dam in a river ecosystem?

- (A) Increased habitats for fish species.
- (B) Reduced water flow downstream.
- (C) Improved air quality in the surrounding area.
- (D) Decreased soil erosion in the region.

29. Students record characteristics of a bean plant. One student's list is shown.

Bean Plant Characteristics

- Thin, climbing stems with small leaves
- Roots growing deep into the soil
- White flowers
- Ten large green beans
- Six small green beans

Which bean plant characteristic is least likely to be inherited?

- (A) Flower color
- (B) Leaf shape
- (C) Type of roots
- (D) Number of beans

30. In which scenarios is light likely to undergo refraction? Select TWO correct answers.

- (A) A student looks through a window to see outside.
- (B) Light reflects off a mirror onto a wall.
- (C) A student watches a shadow move across a wall.
- (D) Light bends when passing through a glass of water.
- (E) A student observes stars through a telescope lens.

16

31. Why does the appearance of constellations change throughout the year?

(A) Earth revolves around the Sun.

(B) Earth rotates on its axis.

(C) The Sun revolves around Earth.

(D) Constellations rotate on their axes.

32. A student is learning about the inner and outer planets of our solar system. Which statements about the inner and outer planets are correct? Select TWO correct answers.

(A) Inner planets are closer to the Sun than outer planets.

(B) Outer planets are smaller and rockier than inner planets.

(C) Inner planets have fewer moons than outer planets.

(D) Outer planets have no atmospheres.

(E) Inner and outer planets are made of the same materials.

33. Which statement best explains why we have seasons on Earth?

(A) The Earth's distance from the Sun changes.

(B) The Earth rotates on its axis.

(C) The Earth's axis is tilted as it revolves around the Sun.

(D) The Sun's energy output varies throughout the year.

34. Which statement explains why we see different constellations at different times of the year?

(A) The stars in the constellations are moving.

(B) Earth's orbit around the Sun changes our view of the stars.

(C) The Sun's light changes the visibility of stars.

(D) Constellations move along with the moon.

35. A student learns that Earth has layers. Which of the following correctly lists these layers from the outermost to the innermost?

(A) Crust, mantle, outer core, inner core.

(B) Mantle, crust, inner core, outer core.

(C) Crust, outer core, mantle, inner core.

(D) Inner core, outer core, mantle, crust.

36. A picture and a description of a wolf and a polar seal are shown in the chart.

• Lives in forests, grasslands, and tundra across North America, Europe, and Asia. • Its diet includes a variety of animals such as deer, elk, moose, and smaller mammals like rabbits and rodents. • Wolves hunt in packs, using teamwork to catch their prey. • They typically produce 4-6 offspring per year, and the offspring stay with the pack for several years. • There are thousands of wolves in the wild, and they are not considered endangered.	• Lives in the icy waters and on the ice floes of the Arctic. • Its diet consists mainly of fish, squid, and other marine organisms. • Polar seals are excellent swimmers and can hold their breath for long periods to dive for food. • They usually produce 1 offspring every year, and the offspring stay with their mother for about a year. • Some estimates show that there are only a few hundred thousand polar seals left in the wild, making them vulnerable to environmental changes and hunting.

What are TWO likely reasons why wolves have a much greater population in the wild than polar seals?

A Wolves live in a wider range of habitats, including forests, grasslands, and tundra, while polar seals are limited to the Arctic region.

B Wolves produce fewer offspring, which means they need less food to sustain their population compared to polar seals.

C Wolves have a varied diet that includes many types of animals, while polar seals primarily eat fish and marine organisms, which may be affected by changes in the Arctic ecosystem.

D Polar seals are better swimmers, which helps them escape predators more effectively than wolves can.

E Wolves are more affected by environmental changes compared to polar seals, whose habitat is impacted by climate change.

37. Lions are apex predators that live in savannah ecosystems. They hunt large herbivores such as zebras and wildebeests. If lions are removed from savannah ecosystems, it can affect the savannah's communities. Which statement BEST predicts the effect of removing lions from savannah ecosystems?

A The variety of different organisms throughout savannah ecosystems will increase.

B Organisms that compete with the lions for food will decrease in numbers.

C Organisms that the lions prey on will increase in numbers.

D The savannah ecosystem will become a desert.

38. A group of animals is shown.

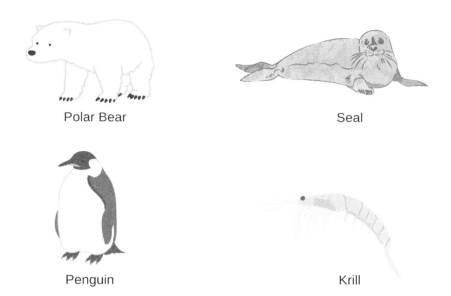

Polar Bear

Seal

Penguin

Krill

Which habitat are these animals BEST suited for?

A A hot desert with sand dunes and cacti.

B A tropical rainforest with dense foliage and high humidity.

C An icy Arctic region with sea ice and cold temperatures.

D A shallow coastal bay with sandy beaches and mangroves.

39. A student is pushing a heavy box across a smooth floor. What change will reduce the amount of force needed to move the box?

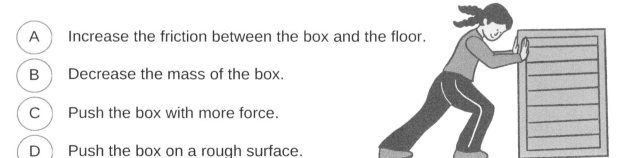

A Increase the friction between the box and the floor.

B Decrease the mass of the box.

C Push the box with more force.

D Push the box on a rough surface.

40. Which of these is an example of potential energy?

(A) A moving car

(B) A stretched rubber band

(C) A running horse

(D) A spinning top

41. Students want to determine how the type of ball affects the distance it rolls on a smooth surface. Which procedure should they follow for their experiment?

(A) Measure the distance rolled by different balls on different surfaces. Conduct three trials for each ball.

(B) Measure the distance rolled by the same ball on different surfaces. Conduct three trials for each surface.

(C) Measure the distance rolled by different balls on the same surface. Conduct three trials for each ball.

(D) Measure the distance rolled by the same ball on the same surface by different students. Conduct three trials for each student.

42. The circuit has five lightbulbs and four switches. If Switch 3 and 4 are closed, which lightbulbs will glow? Write the answer on the line provided. If none of the lightbulbs will glow, write NONE on the line: _____

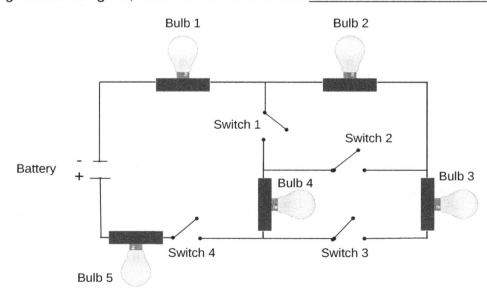

43. A baseball thrown through the air eventually falls back to the ground. What force causes the baseball to fall?

- (A) Wind resistance pushing against the baseball.

- (B) Gravity pulling the baseball downward.

- (C) Friction between the baseball and the air.

- (D) Elastic force from the impact of throwing the baseball.

44. A toy car rolls down a ramp and hits a stack of blocks, causing the blocks to scatter. What force caused the blocks to move?

- (A) Wind pushing against the blocks.

- (B) Gravity pulling the blocks downward.

- (C) Friction between the toy car and the ramp.

- (D) Elastic force from the impact of the toy car.

Answers Practice Test 1

1. D. 1 year
2. A. Mercury
3. B. The Earth's rotation on its axis
4. A. Plankton → fish → seals → sharks
5. C. A series of organisms each dependent on the next as a source of food.
6. A. Phytoplankton
7. D. By using public transport and reducing energy consumption.
8. B. Both animals and plants undergo a series of changes throughout their life cycle that enable them to survive and reproduce.
9. C. Thermal energy
10. A. The iron absorbs heat from the fire.
11. C. The light is refracted by the prism.
    C. The prism bends (refracts) different wavelengths of light in different amounts.
12. C. Friction between the ball and the grass
13. A. The particles have a higher density than water.
14. B. Light reflection
15. C. Water vapor condensed on the grass.
16. B. Use a magnet to attract the nails.
17. D. Place the mixture in a refrigerator to solidify the oil.
18. A. Sample 1 is plastic.
19. D. Bee building a hive.
20. A. Both are formed by underground magma chambers.
21. B. The ice cube will decrease in size.
A. The ice cube absorbs heat from the surroundings, causing it to melt.
22. B. The salt dissolved in the water.
23. A. A fish swims through water.
24. C. 11 hours
25. A. Ecosystem 1
26. B. Igneous rocks
27. B. Aluminum

28. B. Reduced water flow downstream.
29. D. Number of beans
30. A. A student looks through a window to see outside,
    D. Light bends when passing through a glass of water.
31. A. Earth revolves around the sun.
32. A. Inner planets are closer to the sun than outer planets,
    C. Inner planets have fewer moons than outer planets.
33. C. The Earth's axis is tilted as it revolves around the sun.
34. B. Earth's orbit around the sun changes our view of the stars.
35. A. Crust, mantle, outer core, inner core
36. A. Wolves live in a wider range of habitats, including forests, grasslands, and tundra, while polar seals are limited to the Arctic region.
    C. Wolves have a varied diet that includes many types of animals, while polar seals primarily eat fish and marine organisms, which may be affected by changes in the Arctic ecosystem.
37. C. Organisms that the lions prey on will increase in numbers.
38. C. An icy Arctic region with sea ice and cold temperatures.
39. B. Decrease the mass of the box
40. B. A stretched rubber band
41. C. Measure the distance rolled by different balls on the same surface. Conduct three trials for each ball.
42. Bulbs 1, 2, 3, and 5.
43. B. Gravity pulling the baseball downward.
44. D. Elastic force from the impact of the toy car.

23

PRACTICE TEST 2

GET STARTED →

1. How long does it take for the Earth to complete one full rotation on its axis?

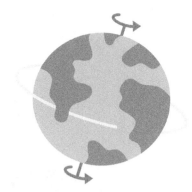

(A) 24 hours

(B) 30 days

(C) 6 months

(D) 1 year

2. How many planets in the solar system have rings?

(A) One

(B) Two

(C) Three

(D) Four

3. Which process describes the water cycle on Earth?

(A) Photosynthesis

(B) Plate tectonics

(C) Evaporation, condensation, and precipitation

(D) Erosion and sedimentation

4. Which food chain accurately represents a pond ecosystem?

(A) Algae → insects → fish → turtles

(B) Turtles → fish → insects → algae

(C) Fish → turtles → algae → insects

(D) Algae → turtles → fish → insects

5. Which of the following animals is a mammal?

    (A) Crocodile

    (B) Dolphin

    (C) Hawk

    (D) Salmon

6. This question has two parts. First, answer Part A. Then, answer Part B.

Part A

A student plants two identical seeds in separate pots. One pot is placed in a sunny window, and the other pot is placed in a dark closet. After a week, the seed in the sunny window has sprouted, but the seed in the closet has not. Which statement BEST explains why the seed in the sunny window sprouted faster?

    (A) The sunny window provides more water to the seed.

    (B) The sunny window has warmer temperatures, which help the seed grow.

    (C) The sunny window protects the seed from insects and pests.

    (D) The sunny window has more nutrients in the soil.

Part B

Which statement BEST explains the answer to Part A?

    (A) Seeds need sunlight to make their food through photosynthesis.

    (B) Seeds need darkness to absorb water and grow roots.

    (C) Seeds need heat to store energy for growth.

    (D) Seeds need nutrients from the soil to sprout roots.

26

7. What process do plants use to convert sunlight into chemical energy as illustrated at the image below?

A Transpiration

B Photosynthesis

C Erosion

D Germination

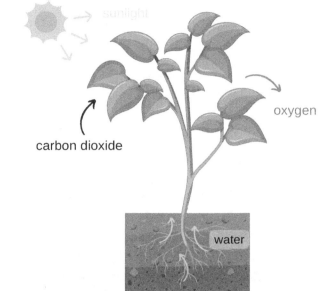

8. Students observe the diagram below showing the life cycle of silkworms. What do silkworms spin to create their cocoons?

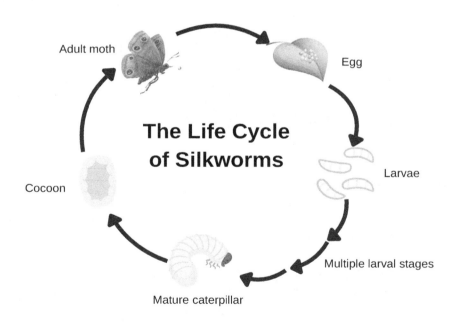

A Silk thread

B Wax

C Cotton

D Wool

9. A student observed the time it took for a wet towel to dry after being hung outside on a clothesline. Which kind of energy primarily causes the water in the towel to evaporate?

A Electrical energy from nearby power lines.

B Chemical energy from the air.

C Thermal energy from the sun.

D Gravitational energy from the Earth.

10. A student places a metal spoon in a cup of hot soup. Which type of energy causes the spoon to become warm?

A Mechanical energy from stirring.

B Electrical energy from the microwave.

C Chemical energy from the soup.

D Thermal energy from the hot soup.

11. During a thunderstorm, a student sees lightning. What causes the thunderclap that follows shortly afterward?

A Lightning absorbs heat from the air.

B Lightning reflects sound waves.

C Lightning generates sound waves.

D Lighting creates a vacuum.

12. Which of the following is an example of kinetic energy?

- (A) A book sitting on a shelf
- (B) A stretched bowstring
- (C) A moving car
- (D) A compressed spring

13. Students observe the picture below where two different liquids are poured into a test tube, forming two phases.

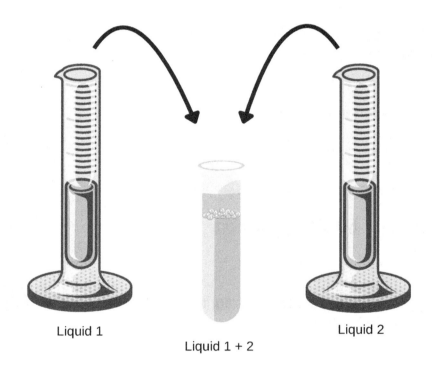

Liquid 1

Liquid 1 + 2

Liquid 2

Which conclusion can be made from image?

- (A) Liquid 1 has a lower density than liquid 2.
- (B) Liquid 2 has a lower density than liquid 1.
- (C) Liquid 1 and 2 have the same density.
- (D) Liquid 1 is soluble in liquid 2.

14. A helium-filled balloon is released and begins to rise. What force primarily causes the balloon to eventually come back down to the ground?

A. Air pressure from the surrounding atmosphere.

B. Gravity pulling the balloon downward.

C. Electrostatic force attracting the balloon to the ground.

D. Force from the helium inside the balloon.

15. What happens when the north poles of two magnets are brought close together?

A. They attract each other.

B. They repel each other.

C. They become neutral.

D. Nothing happens.

16. In an experiment, a student mixes sugar and water. How can the student separate the sugar from the water?

A. Use a magnet to attract the sugar particles.

B. Heat the mixture until the sugar crystallizes.

C. Pour the mixture through filter paper.

D. Allow the water to evaporate, leaving behind the sugar.

17. A student accidentally spills a mixture of ink and water. How can the student separate the ink from the water?

(A) Dissolve the mixture in more water and then filter it.

(B) Use a magnet to attract the ink particles.

(C) Pour the mixture through filter paper.

(D) Allow the water to evaporate, leaving behind the ink.

18. A table of the properties of four different samples of matter is shown.

Sample	Conducts Electricity	Conducts Heat	Soluble in Water	Physical State at Room Temperature
1	No	No	No	Solid
2	Yes	Yes	No	Solid
3	No	Yes	Yes	Liquid
4	Yes	Yes	No	Liquid

Which answer is correct for sample 2?

(A) Sample 2 is plastic.

(B) Sample 2 is iron.

(C) Sample 2 is alcohol.

(D) Sample 2 is oxygen.

19. How can fossils help scientists understand past climates?

(A) By showing weather patterns directly.

(B) By indicating the presence of ancient humans.

(C) By revealing what kinds of plants and animals lived in an area.

(D) By containing water samples from the past.

31

20. Caves and sinkholes are geological formations commonly found in karst landscapes. Which statement best describes how caves and sinkholes are similar?

- (A) Both are formed by volcanic activity.
- (B) Both are created by deposition of sedimentary rocks.
- (C) Both are carved out by chemical weathering.
- (D) Both are results of glacier movements.

21. In our solar system, what is the order of the planets from the sun?

- (A) Earth is the first planet, and Mars is the second.
- (B) Mercury is the first planet, and Venus is the second.
- (C) Mars is the first planet, and Jupiter is the second.
- (D) Jupiter is the first planet, and Saturn is the second.

22. A student dropped a drop of ink into a glass of water and observed that the ink spread throughout the water, turning it blue. What most likely happened to the ink?

- (A) The ink evaporated into the air.
- (B) The ink dissolved in the water.
- (C) The ink sank to the bottom of the glass.
- (D) The ink froze in the cold water.

23. Imagine you are studying a species of mammals that live in cold Arctic regions. You observe the following characteristics:

- Thick fur coat
- A layer of blubber under the skin
- Small, rounded ears
- Large, padded paws
- Diet primarily consists of seals and fish

Based on these characteristics, which habitat do you think this mammal is most likely adapted to live in?

- A) Rainforest
- B) Arctic Tundra
- C) Desert
- D) Grassland

24. Why are the days longer during the summer compared to winter?

- A) The Earth moves closer to the Sun during the summer.
- B) The Earth tilts on its axis, causing more direct sunlight in one hemisphere.
- C) The Sun becomes larger in the sky during the summer.
- D) The Earth rotates more slowly during the summer.

25. Silkworms are known for their ability to produce silk used in textiles. Which habitat below would be most suitable for silkworms to thrive?

- A) Temperate forests with moderate rainfall and rich soil.
- B) Hot deserts with sandy and dry soil.
- C) Tropical rainforests with high humidity and abundant vegetation.
- D) Polar regions with icy conditions and sparse vegetation.

33

26. A three-step process is shown:

Evaporation → Condensation → Precipitation

Which of these are most likely formed by the process shown?

- A) Clouds
- B) Earthquakes
- C) Volcanoes
- D) Sedimentary rocks

27. A group of students is given four small blocks of the same size and instructed to place them in a tank of liquid. One block floats to the surface of the liquid. Two of the blocks float in the middle of the tank under the surface of the liquid. The last block sinks to the bottom of the tank.

Which conclusion is best supported by what the students observed?

- A) Two of the four blocks are soluble in the liquid
- B) All four blocks have different weights
- C) Each block is made of a different type of wood
- D) One of the blocks is less dense than the other three.

28. Which consequence would most likely result from the construction of a new airport in a rural area?

- A) Increased green space for wildlife.
- B) Decreased levels of noise pollution.
- C) Disruption of local wildlife habitats.
- D) Enhanced air quality in the region.

34

29. Students observe different types of vegetables in a garden. They focus on carrots and record their characteristics:

Carrot Characteristics:
- Edible taproot with orange color.
- Feathery leaves growing from the stem.
- Roots extending deep into the soil.
- Biennial plant with flowers in the second year.
- Grows best in loose, sandy soil.

Which TWO characteristics of carrots are most likely inherited?

- (A) Root depth
- (B) Leaf shape
- (C) Flowering habit
- (D) Root color

30. Which activities involve light being refracted?

- (A) A student looks at a digital clock.
- (B) Light passes through a magnifying glass.
- (C) A student watches clouds drift across the sky.
- (D) A student sees their shadow on a sunny day.

31. What is the reason for the changing length of daylight hours throughout the year?

- (A) Earth revolves around the sun.
- (B) Earth rotates on its axis.
- (C) The sun revolves around Earth.
- (D) Daylight hours are constant throughout the year.

32. A student is comparing the features of different types of stars. Which statements about stars are correct? Select TWO correct answers.

(A) Red giants are larger than white dwarfs.

(B) White dwarfs are hotter than red giants.

(C) All stars are the same size.

(D) Stars do not produce light or heat.

(E) Stars are made of solid materials like planets.

33. Why do stars appear to twinkle when we look at them from Earth?

(A) Stars are constantly changing in brightness.

(B) Earth's atmosphere distorts the light from stars.

(C) Stars move quickly in space.

(D) The sun's light interferes with starlight.

34. A student looks at the night sky and sees the Milky Way. What is the Milky Way?

(A) A galaxy that includes our solar system.

(B) A star close to Earth.

(C) A constellation that appears in winter.

(D) A meteor shower that happens annually.

35. Which statement best describes why the Earth is habitable for humans?

A Earth is the closest planet to the sun.

B Earth has a thick atmosphere with oxygen.

C Earth rotates once every 24 hours.

D Earth has large polar ice caps.

36. A picture and a description of a mouse and a squirrel are shown in the chart.

• Lives in diverse habitats including forests, grasslands, agricultural areas, and urban settings worldwide. • Its diet consists of seeds, grains, fruits, and insects. • Mice are small and can hide in small spaces to escape predators. • They typically produce multiple litters per year, each containing 5-10 offspring. • Mice are very common and have large populations in the wild.	• Lives in forests, parks, and urban areas with trees worldwide. • Its diet primarily includes nuts, seeds, fruits, and occasionally insects. • Squirrels are agile climbers and can leap between branches to escape predators. • They typically produce 1-2 litters per year, each containing 2-8 offspring. • Squirrels are common, but their populations can be affected by habitat destruction and food availability.

What are TWO likely reasons why mice have a much greater population in the wild than squirrels?

A Mice live in a wider range of habitats, including forests, grasslands, agricultural areas, and urban settings, while squirrels are primarily found in areas with trees.

B Mice produce fewer offspring per year compared to squirrels, which means they need less food to sustain their population.

C Mice have a more diverse diet that includes seeds, grains, fruits, and insects, while squirrels primarily eat nuts, seeds, and fruits.

D Squirrels are agile climbers, which helps them escape predators more effectively than mice can.

E Mice are significantly larger than squirrels, allowing them to dominate their habitats.

37

37. What is the main function of the leaves on a plant?

(A) To absorb water

(B) To produce seeds

(C) To capture sunlight for photosynthesis

(D) To anchor the plant

38. A group of animals is shown.

Trout

Heron

Beaver

Which habitat are these animals BEST suited for?

(A) A deep-sea trench with low temperatures and high pressure.

(B) A fast-flowing river with rocky rapids and waterfalls.

(C) A deciduous forest with rich soil and four distinct seasons.

(D) A coastal mangrove forest with brackish water and tangled roots.

39. Students are experimenting with pulling a wagon up a hill. What change will reduce the force needed to pull the wagon up the hill?

(A) Increase the weight of the wagon.

(B) Decrease the steepness of the hill.

(C) Pull the wagon faster.

(D) Use a shorter rope.

40. Which type of energy does a flashlight use to make light?

- A) Kinetic energy
- B) Solar energy
- C) Electrical energy
- D) Chemical energy

41. What type of energy does a windmill convert into electrical energy?

- A) Kinetic energy
- B) Thermal energy
- C) Potential energy
- D) Mechanical energy

42. When you rub your hands together on a cold day, what type of energy is produced, warming up your hands?

- A) Electrical energy
- B) Solar energy
- C) Mechanical energy
- D) Chemical energy

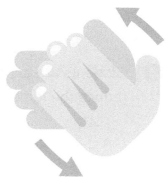

43. Students are testing how the size of a parachute affects the speed it falls from a height. Which procedure should they follow for their experiment?

(A) Measure the speed of descent for parachutes of different sizes. Conduct three trials for each parachute.

(B) Measure the speed of descent for the same parachute from different heights. Conduct three trials for each height.

(C) Measure the speed of descent for parachutes of different sizes on different days. Conduct three trials for each size.

(D) Measure the speed of descent for the same parachute from the same height by different students. Conduct three trials for each student.

44. The circuit has five lightbulbs and four switches. If Switch 2 and 3 are closed, which lightbulbs will glow? Write the answer on the line provided. If none of the lightbulbs will glow, write NONE on the line: _____

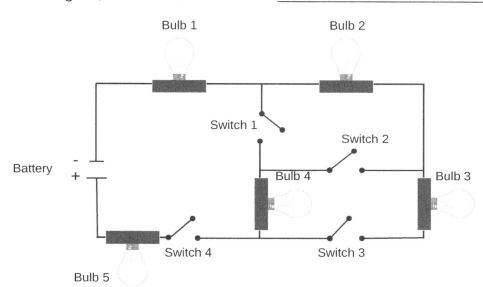

Answers Test Practice 2

1. A. 24 hours
2. D. Four
3. C. Evaporation, condensation, and precipitation.
4. A. Algae → insects → fish → turtles
5. B. Dolphin
6. B. The sunny window has warmer temperatures, which help the seed grow.
      A. Seeds need sunlight to make their food through photosynthesis.
7. B. Photosynthesis
8. A. Silk threads
9. C. Thermal energy from the sun.
10. D. Thermal energy from the hot soup.
11. C. Lightning generates sound waves.
12. C. A moving car
13. B. Liquid 2 has a lower density than liquid 1.
14. B. Gravity pulling the balloon downward.
15. B. They repel each other.
16. D. Allow the water to evaporate, leaving behind the sugar.
17. D. Allow the water to evaporate, leaving behind the ink.
18. B. Sample 2 is iron.
19. C. By revealing what kinds of plants and animals lived in an area.
20. C. Both are carved out by chemical weathering.
21. B. Mercury is the first planet, and Venus is the second.
22. B. The ink dissolved in the water.
23. B. Arctic Tundra
24. B. The Earth tilts on its axis, causing more direct sunlight in one hemisphere.
25. C. Tropical rainforests with high humidity and abundant vegetation.

26. A. Clouds
27. D. One of the blocks is less dense than the other three.
28. C. Disruption of local wildlife habitats.
29. B. Leaf shape
      D. Root color
30. B. Light passes through a magnifying glass.
31. A. Earth revolves around the sun.
32. A. Red giants are larger than white dwarfs.
      B. White dwarfs are hotter than red giants.
33. B. Earth's atmosphere distorts the light from stars.
34. A. A galaxy that includes our solar system.
35. B. Earth has a thick atmosphere with oxygen.
36. A. Mice live in a wider range of habitats, including forests, grasslands, agricultural areas, and urban settings, while squirrels are primarily found in areas with trees.
      C. Mice have a more diverse diet that includes seeds, grains, fruits, and insects, while squirrels primarily eat nuts, seeds, and fruits.
37. C. To capture sunlight for photosynthesis.
38. B. A fast-flowing river with rocky rapids and waterfalls.
39. B. Decrease the steepness of the hill.
40. C. Electrical energy
41. A. Kinetic energy
42. C. Mechanical energy
43. A. Measure the speed of descent for parachutes of different sizes. Conduct three trials for each parachute.
44. NONE

PRACTICE TEST 3

GET STARTED $\longrightarrow$

1. The Earth revolves around the Sun. What shape is the Earth's orbit around the Sun?

A) Circular

B) Elliptical

C) Rectangular

D) Triangular

2. What is the largest planet in our solar system by diameter?

A) Jupiter

B) Saturn

C) Uranus

D) Neptune

3. What is the most abundant gas in the Earth's atmosphere?

A) Oxygen

B) Carbon Dioxide

C) Nitrogen

D) Argon

4. Which of the following food chains correctly shows the flow of energy in a grassland ecosystem?

A   Grass → rabbits → foxes → eagles

B   Eagles → foxes → rabbits → grass

C   Rabbits → eagles → foxes → grass

D   Grass → foxes → eagles → rabbits

5. What is the main cause of global warming?

A   Volcanic eruptions and other natural phenomena.

B   Natural climate cycles that warm and cool the Earth.

C   Increased levels of greenhouse gases from human activities.

D   Solar flares, electromagnetic radiation, and similar energies.

6. In a desert ecosystem, what is the primary source of energy?

A   Cacti

B   Insects

C   Birds

D   Sunlight

7. How do plants primarily obtain carbon dioxide for photosynthesis?

A Through their roots.

B Through their leaves.

C Through their stems.

D Through their flowers.

8. Students observe a chicken life cycle diagram. What is the first stage in the life cycle of a chicken?

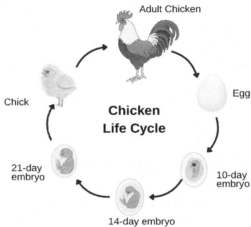

A Chick

B Adult

C Egg

D Embryo

9. During a thunderstorm, a student sees a flash of lightning. Which form of energy causes the lightning to occur?

A Mechanical energy from wind.

B Electrical energy from clouds.

C Chemical energy from rainwater.

D Thermal energy from the Sun.

10. During a foggy night walk, a student noticed the reflection of the street lights on the fog. What is the reason the light from the lamp becomes more visible in the fog?

- (A) The fog particles reflect the light.
- (B) The light is absorbed by the fog particles.
- (C) The light passes through fog without any interaction.
- (D) The light from the lamp changes color in the fog.

11. Which of the following objects would have the most kinetic energy?

- (A) A car parked in a garage.
- (B) A bicycle leaning against a wall.
- (C) A rolling soccer ball.
- (D) A rock resting on the ground.

12. Which type of energy is produced by vibrating objects?

- (A) Electrical energy
- (B) Chemical energy
- (C) Sound energy
- (D) Nuclear energy

13. Students observe the picture below where particles of an unknown material are added to pure water. After mixing, the particles float to the top of the container.

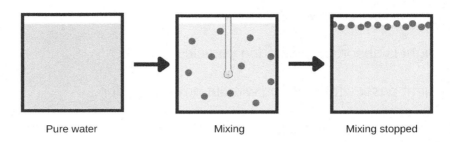

Pure water   Mixing   Mixing stopped

Which conclusion can be made from image?

(A) The particles have a higher density than water.

(B) The particles have a lower density than water.

(C) The particles have the same density as water.

(D) The particles are soluble in water.

14. Which of these materials would be the best conductor of electricity?

(A) Rubber

(B) Plastic

(C) Copper

(D) Wood

15. What is the purpose of a switch in an electrical circuit?

(A) To store electricity.

(B) To control the flow of electricity.

(C) To measure electricity.

(D) To generate electricity.

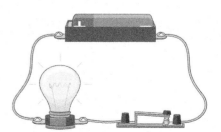

16. Which of the following is an example of a chemical change?

    (A) Melting ice

    (B) Cutting paper

    (C) Burning wood

    (D) Dissolving salt in water

17. A student prepares a mixture of tea leaves and water. What is the fastest way for the student to separate the tea leaves from the water?

    (A) Use a magnet to attract the tea leaves.

    (B) Heat the mixture until the tea leaves settle at the bottom.

    (C) Pour the mixture through filter paper.

    (D) Allow the water to evaporate, leaving behind the tea leaves.

18. A table of the properties of four different samples of matter is shown.

Sample	Conducts Electricity	Conducts Heat	Soluble in Water	Physical State at Room Temperature
1	No	No	No	Solid
2	Yes	Yes	No	Solid
3	No	Yes	Yes	Liquid
4	Yes	Yes	No	Liquid

Which answer is correct for sample 3?

    (A) Sample 3 is plastic.

    (B) Sample 3 is iron.

    (C) Sample 3 is alcohol.

    (D) Sample 3 is oxygen.

19. How are fossils typically formed?

A) When plants or animals are buried quickly by sediment.

B) When plants or animals dry out in the sun.

C) When organisms are frozen in ice.

D) When organisms decompose completely.

20. Deltas and estuaries are coastal landforms shaped by water. Which statement best describes how deltas and estuaries are similar?

A) Both are formed by glacial erosion.

B) Both are influenced by tidal currents.

C) Both are results of volcanic eruptions.

D) Both are affected by seismic activity.

21. What is the Sun mainly made of?

A) Rock

B) Ice

C) Gas

D) Metal

22. A student compares the flow of water through four different types of sand. The setup and results of the investigation are shown in the table.

The student used this procedure to perform the investigation:

1. Place 100 grams of each type of sand into one of the funnels with a coffee filter.
2. Slowly pour 100 milliliters of water onto the sand in each funnel.
3. Allow the water in each funnel to drain for 30 minutes.
4. Record the amount of water in each beaker.
5. Subtract the amount of water in each beaker from 100 mL and record this number as the amount remaining in the funnel.

Sand Investigation Results

Type of Sand	Volume of Water Added (mL)	Water Collected in Beaker	Water Remaining in Funnel
Beach Sand	100	20	80
Desert Sand	100	49	51
River Sand	100	76	24
Volcanic Sand	100	19	81

Based on the investigation's results, answer the questions below.

Which type of sand retained the most water after 30 minutes?

A Beach Sand

B Desert Sand

C River Sand

D Volcanic Sand

23. Please refer to the previous question. Which type of sand allowed the most water to pass through into the beaker?

- (A) Beach Sand
- (B) Desert Sand
- (C) River Sand
- (D) Volcanic Sand

24. A student drew the following pictures to show the day-night cycle of Earth.

Sunrise: 6:15 AM
Sunset: 7:15 PM

Based on the pictures, how many hours of the daytime is in a day-night cycle?

- (A) 12 hours
- (B) 13 hours
- (C) 14 hours
- (D) 24 hours

25. Bengal tigers are large carnivorous cats known for their distinctive orange coat with black stripes. They primarily inhabit dense forests and grasslands, hunting large prey such as deer and wild boar.

Characteristics of Four Habitats

Habitat	Temperature	Yearly Precipitation	Soil
1	Hot and humid year-round	Heavy rainfall	Nutrient-rich soil
2	Moderate with distinct seasons	Evenly distributed rainfall	Loamy, fertile soil
3	Cold winters and mild summers	Low precipitation	Rocky, well-drained soil
4	Dry and arid year-round	Very low precipitation	Sandy, nutrient-poor soil

In which habitat would Bengal tigers be most likely to thrive?

A) Habitat 1

B) Habitat 2

C) Habitat 3

D) Habitat 4

26. A three-step process is shown:

Weathering → Erosion → Deposition

Which of these are most likely formed by the process shown?

A) Volcanic islands

B) River deltas

C) Craters

D) Metamorphic rocks

27. Which of the following materials is known for its hardness and is often used in cutting tools?

- (A) Wood
- (B) Diamond
- (C) Plastic
- (D) Clay

28. Which effect would most likely occur if a large shopping mall were built in an ecosystem?

- (A) Competition for food among animals would decrease.
- (B) Natural habitats for wildlife would be destroyed.
- (C) Noise pollution would decrease.
- (D) Water quality in nearby streams would improve.

29. Which of the following is a non-renewable resource?

- (A) Solar energy
- (B) Wind energy
- (C) Coal
- (D) Water

30. Which situations involve light being refracted? Select TWO correct answers.

(A) A student views a fish in an aquarium.

(B) Light passes through a prism, creating a spectrum.

(C) A student observes their reflection in a spoon.

(D) Sunlight passes through a window into a dark room.

(E) Light travels through a magnifying glass to ignite paper.

31. What is the primary reason why the moon appears to change shape throughout the month?

(A) The moon revolves around Earth.

(B) The moon rotates on its axis.

(C) Earth rotates on its axis.

(D) The Sun revolves around Earth.

32. A student is studying the characteristics of planets and stars. Which statements about planets and stars are correct? Select TWO correct answers.

(A) Planets orbit stars.

(B) Stars are typically smaller than planets.

(C) Stars produce light, while planets reflect light.

(D) Planets are made entirely of gases.

(E) Both planets and stars have the same temperature.

33. A student is learning about the phases of the moon. Which of the following shows the correct sequence of the moon's phases?

(A) New moon, waxing crescent, first quarter, full moon

(B) Full moon, third quarter, waning crescent, new moon

(C) First quarter, waxing crescent, full moon, new moon

(D) Full moon, waxing crescent, first quarter, new moon

34. A student observes a solar eclipse. What is happening during a solar eclipse?

(A) The Earth is between the Sun and the moon.

(B) The moon is between the Sun and the Earth.

(C) The Sun is between the Earth and the moon.

(D) The moon and the Sun are on opposite sides of Earth.

35. What is the smallest unit of an element that still has the properties of that element?

(A) Atom

(B) Molecule

(C) Compound

(D) Cell

36. This question has two parts. First, answer Part A. Then, answer Part B.

Part A

A student observes two animals: a lion and a cheetah. Which statement BEST describes a key difference between lions and cheetahs?

(A) Cheetahs are social animals that live in prides and hunt cooperatively, while lions are solitary hunters.

(B) Lions have spots on their fur for camouflage in grasslands, while cheetahs have a distinct coat pattern for identification.

(C) Lions hunt by stalking their prey and ambushing it in groups, while cheetahs rely on their speed for chasing and catching prey.

(D) Lions have retractable claws for climbing trees, while cheetahs have non-retractable claws for gripping the ground.

Part B

Based on your answer to Part A, which statement BEST explains a potential disadvantage of the behavior or adaptation described?

(A) Lions' ability to camouflage helps them blend into their surroundings to surprise prey.

(B) Cheetahs' reliance on speed makes them vulnerable to injuries during high-speed pursuits.

(C) Lions' stalking behavior requires them to expend more energy compared to cheetahs' quick bursts of speed.

(D) Cheetahs' solitary hunting makes them less efficient in taking down larger prey compared to the lions' cooperative efforts.

37. What do we call a community of living organisms and their physical environment?

(A) Environment

(B) Habitat

(C) Ecosystem

(D) Biome

56

38. A group of animals is shown.

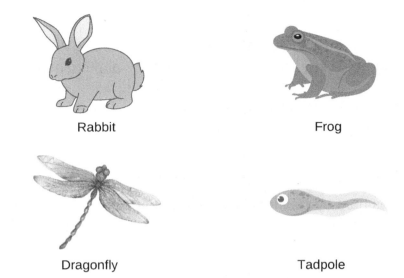

Rabbit

Frog

Dragonfly

Tadpole

Which habitat are these animals BEST suited for?

A. A dense rainforest with tall trees and thick underbrush.

B. A sandy desert with extreme temperature variations.

C. A freshwater pond with aquatic plants and insects.

D. A cold mountain stream with rocky banks.

39. Students are experimenting with different slopes for their toy cars. The cars start from rest at the top of the ramp. What change to the ramp slope will reduce the force required to move the cars?

A. Decrease the steepness of the ramp.

B. Increase the steepness of the ramp.

C. Add weight to the toy cars.

D. Use a longer ramp.

40. When you throw a ball into the air, what force brings it back down to the ground?

(A) Air resistance

(B) Magnetism

(C) Gravity

(D) Friction

41. When you push a swing, what force brings it back towards you after it swings away?

(A) Magnetism

(B) Gravity

(C) Air resistance

(D) Tension

42. Students want to investigate how the height of a ramp affects the distance a toy car travels. Which procedure should they follow for their experiment?

(A) Measure the distance traveled by the toy car using ramps of different heights. Conduct three trials for each height.

(B) Measure the distance traveled by three different toy cars using the same ramp height. Conduct trials for each car.

(C) Measure the distance traveled by the toy car on different surfaces using the same ramp height. Conduct three trials for each surface.

(D) Measure the distance traveled by the toy car on the same ramp height by different students. Conduct three trials for each student.

43. The circuit has five lightbulbs and four switches. If Switch 1 and 4 are closed, which lightbulbs will glow? Write the answer on the line provided. If none of the lightbulbs will glow, write NONE on the line: _____

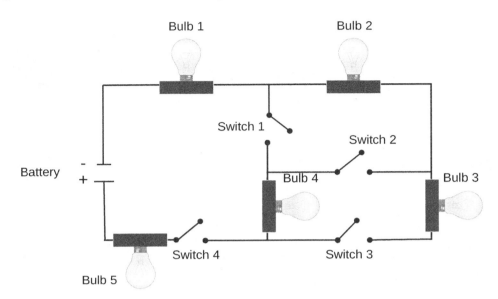

44. What happens when a ball is dropped on a hard surface?

(A) It stops immediately.

(B) It continues to bounce indefinitely.

(C) It bounces back due to elastic force.

(D) It rolls away.

Answers Practice Test 3

1. B. Elliptical
2. A. Jupiter
3. C. Nitrogen
4. A. Grass → rabbits → foxes → eagles
5. C. Increased levels of greenhouse gases from human activities.
6. D. Sunlight
7. B. Through their leaves.
8. C. Egg
9. B. Electrical energy from clouds.
10. A. The fog particles reflect the light.
11. C. A rolling soccer ball.
12. C. Sound energy
13. B. The particles have a lower density than water.
14. C. Copper
15. B. To control the flow of electricity.
16. C. Burning wood
17. C. Pour the mixture through filter paper.
18. C. Sample 3 is alcohol.
19. A. When plants or animals are buried quickly by sediment.
20. B. Both are influenced by tidal currents.
21. C. Gas
22. Question 1: D. Volcanic Sand
23. C. River sand
24. B. 13 hours
25. A. Habitat 1
26. C. River deltas
27. B. Diamond

28. B. Natural habitats for wildlife would be destroyed.
29. C. Coal
30. B. Light passes through a prism, creating a spectrum.
    C. A student observes their reflection in a spoon.
31. A. The moon revolves around Earth.
32. A. Planets orbit stars.
    C. Stars produce light, while planets reflect light.
33. A. New moon, waxing crescent, first quarter, full moon
34. B. The moon is between the sun and the Earth.
35. A. Atom
36. C. Lions hunt by stalking their prey and ambushing it in groups, while cheetahs rely on their speed for chasing and catching prey.
    D. Cheetahs' solitary hunting makes them less efficient in taking down larger prey compared to the lions' cooperative efforts.
37. C. Ecosystem
38. A. A dense rainforest with tall trees and thick underbrush.
39. C. Add weight to the toy cars
40. C. Gravity
41. B. Gravity
42. A. Measure the distance traveled by the toy car using ramps of different heights. Conduct three trials for each height.
43. Bulbs 1 and 5.
44. C. It bounces back due to elastic force.

PRACTICE TEST 4

GET STARTED →

1. What is the smallest planet in our solar system by diameter?

(A) Mercury

(B) Venus

(C) Mars

(D) Pluto

2. The Earth has a natural satellite. What is it called?

(A) Sun

(B) Mars

(C) Moon

(D) Venus

3. Which force keeps the Earth in orbit around the Sun?

(A) Electromagnetic force

(B) Gravitational force

(C) Nuclear force

(D) Frictional force

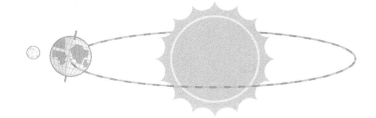

4. Why do you think some animals have bright colors?

(A) To hide from predators.

(B) To attract mates.

(C) To scare away prey.

(D) To camouflage.

5. Why do you think plants have different types of leaves (e.g., broad, needle-like, spiky)?

(A) To make them look interesting.

(B) To help them catch insects.

(C) To adapt to different environments.

(D) To scare away animals.

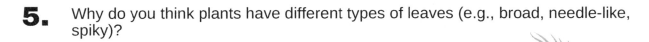

6. In a grassland ecosystem, what is the primary source of energy?

(A) Bison

(B) Grass

(C) Birds

(D) Wind

7. Answer the question with the help of the following image. What gas is released into the atmosphere as a byproduct of photosynthesis?

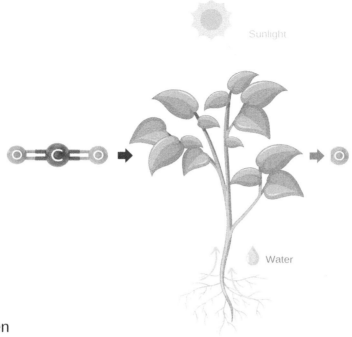

(A) Oxygen

(B) Nitrogen

(C) Carbon dioxide

(D) Methane

8. Students observe a diagram showing the life cycle of ferns. Where do ferns produce their spores?

(A) On the leaves.

(B) In flowers.

(C) In cones.

(D) On the stems.

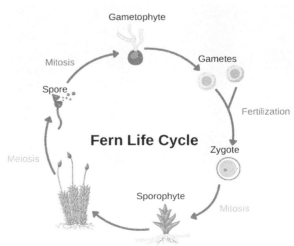

9. A student rubs two sticks together to start a fire while camping. Which type of energy is primarily responsible for igniting the sticks?

A Nuclear energy from the ground.

B Electrical energy from a nearby generator.

C Chemical energy from friction.

D Thermal energy from the air.

10. How does a trampoline demonstrate elastic force?

A By absorbing sound.

B By storing energy and bouncing back.

C By attracting objects.

D By conducting electricity.

11. Students observe the image below where two different liquids are poured into the same container. Which conclusion can be made from the image?

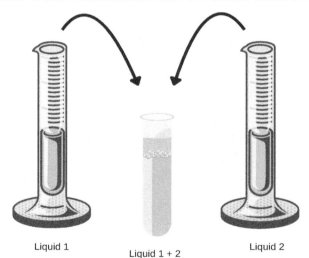

Liquid 1   Liquid 1 + 2   Liquid 2

A The different liquids could be water and oil.

B The different liquids could be water and alcohol.

C Liquid 1 is soluble in liquid 2.

D Two different liquids could be water and dishwashing soap.

12. This question has two parts. First, answer Part A. Then, based on your answer to Part A, answer Part B.

Part A
A student examines two plants: a dandelion and an oak tree. Which statement BEST describes a key difference between dandelions and oak trees in their reproduction?

A. Dandelions reproduce through seeds that disperse in the wind, while oak trees reproduce through acorns that fall to the ground.

B. Dandelions reproduce through acorns that fall to the ground, while oak trees reproduce through seeds that disperse in the wind.

C. Dandelions and oak trees reproduce through spores released from their leaves, but dandelions grow faster in moist soil.

D. Dandelions and oak trees are similar in reproduction methods, but dandelions have broader leaves that capture more sunlight for photosynthesis.

Part B
Based on your answer to Part A, which statement BEST explains how this difference in reproduction helps each plant species survive?

A. Dandelions' ability to disperse seeds in the wind allows them to colonize new areas quickly and compete with other plants for resources.

B. Oak trees' production of acorns provides a food source for animals such as squirrels and deer, ensuring widespread seed dispersal.

C. Dandelions' slow growth does not allow them to spread seeds fast compared to oak trees.

D. Oak trees' needle-like leaves capture less sunlight, making them unable to grow taller and overshadow other plants in dense forest environments.

13. Which of the following is a characteristic of acids?

A. Sour taste.

B. Bitter taste.

C. Slippery feel.

D. Red litmus paper turns blue.

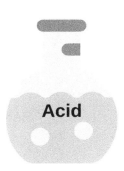

Acid

14. If you place a cold spoon in a hot cup of soup, what will happen to the temperature of the spoon and the soup?

(A) The spoon will get colder, and the soup will stay the same.

(B) The spoon will get warmer, and the soup will get cooler.

(C) The spoon and soup will both get warmer.

(D) The spoon and soup will both get cooler.

15. In a recycling project, a student mixes plastic beads and metal screws. How can the student separate the plastic beads from the metal screws?

(A) Dissolve the mixture in water and then filter it.

(B) Use a magnet to attract the metal screws.

(C) Heat the mixture until the plastic beads melt.

(D) Pour the mixture through filter paper to separate.

16. A table of the properties of four different samples of matter is shown.

Sample	Conducts Electricity	Conducts Heat	Soluble in Water	Physical State at Room Temperature
1	No	No	No	Solid
2	Yes	Yes	No	Solid
3	No	Yes	Yes	Liquid
4	Yes	Yes	No	Liquid

Which answer is correct for sample 4?

(A) Sample 4 is plastic.

(B) Sample 4 is iron.

(C) Sample 4 is alcohol.

(D) Sample 4 is mercury.

17. What is the main characteristic of mammals?

A They lay eggs.

B They have hair or fur and produce milk for their young.

C They have scales.

D They can fly.

18. Plateaus and buttes are elevated landforms found in various regions. Which statement best describes how plateaus and buttes are similar?

A Both are formed by volcanic ash deposits.

B Both are shaped by uplift and erosion.

C Both are remnants of ancient sea beds.

D Both are results of underground lava flows.

19. In modern astronomy, scientists study Earth and Mars using advanced telescopes. What are the positions of these planets in relation to the Sun?

A Earth is the planet closest to the Sun, and Mars is the second planet from the Sun.

B Earth is the second planet from the Sun, and Mars is the third planet from the Sun.

C Mars is the planet closest to the Sun, and Earth is the second planet from the Sun.

D Earth is the third planet from the Sun, and Mars is the fourth planet from the Sun.

20. A student stirred a sugar cube into a cup of hot coffee. After stirring, the student noticed that the coffee tasted sweeter. What most likely happened to the sugar cube?

- (A) The sugar cube turned into steam and disappeared.
- (B) The sugar cube broke into smaller pieces.
- (C) The sugar cube dissolved in the coffee.
- (D) The sugar cube sank to the bottom of the cup.

21. Imagine you are studying a plant species found in wetlands. You observe the following characteristics:

- Broad, flat leaves
- Extensive root system
- Ability to float on water
- White flowers that bloom at night
- Seeds dispersed by water currents

Based on these characteristics, which habitat do you think this plant is most likely adapted to live in?

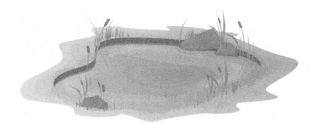

- (A) Desert
- (B) Rainforest
- (C) Wetlands
- (D) Grassland

22. Why do days and nights have almost equal length during the equinoxes?

- (A) The Earth's axis is perpendicular to its orbit around the Sun.
- (B) The Earth is closest to the Sun during the equinoxes.
- (C) The Moon is in a specific position that balances day and night.
- (D) The Sun's energy is equally distributed around the Earth during the equinoxes.

69

23. Polar bears are large carnivorous mammals known for their thick fur and ability to survive in harsh cold climates. In which habitat are polar bears most likely to be found?

(A) Tropical rainforests with dense vegetation.

(B) Arctic regions with sea ice and tundra.

(C) Deserts with extreme temperatures and sparse vegetation.

(D) Grasslands with moderate temperatures and open plains.

24. A three-step process is shown:

Uplift → Weathering → Erosion

Which of these are most likely formed by the process shown?

(A) Fossils

(B) Mountains

(C) Valleys

(D) Lava flows

25. Why do you think some substances dissolve in water while others do not?

(A) Because they like to stay dry.

(B) Because they are afraid of water.

(C) Because they are made of different molecules.

(D) Because they want to hide.

26. What would most likely happen if a forest area was cleared to build residential housing?

A Biodiversity in the area would increase.

B Soil erosion would decrease.

C Animal migration routes would be disrupted.

D Water levels in local rivers would rise.

27. Students observe different types of birds in a wetland. They focus on ducks and record their characteristics:

Duck Characteristics:
- Webbed feet for swimming
- Waterproof feathers for floating
- Omnivorous diet of aquatic plants, insects, and small fish
- Nests near water in reeds or grasses
- Migration to warmer areas in winter

Why do ducks have webbed feet?

A To climb trees.

B To attract mates.

C To swim and dive for food.

D To dig burrows.

28. What do you think happens when you mix vinegar (acetic acid) and baking soda (sodium bicarbonate)?

A They explode.

B They turn into a solid.

C They create bubbles and fizz.

D They turn into water.

29. What causes the apparent movement of stars across the night sky?

- A) Earth revolves around the Sun.
- B) Earth rotates on its axis.
- C) The Sun revolves around Earth.
- D) Stars rotate on their axes.

30. A student is observing the characteristics of comets and asteroids. Which statements about comets and asteroids are correct? Select TWO correct answers.

- A) Comets are primarily made of ice and dust.
- B) Asteroids produce light like stars.
- C) Both comets and asteroids orbit the Sun.
- D) Comets are only found in the asteroid belt.
- E) Asteroids have tails that grow when they approach the Sun.

31. A student is studying the planets in our solar system. Which statements about the planets are correct? Select TWO correct answers.

- A) Mars is known as the Red Planet.
- B) Jupiter is the smallest planet.
- C) Venus has a surface covered with water.
- D) Saturn is famous for its rings.
- E) Mercury is the furthest planet from the Sun.

32. What causes day and night on Earth?

A The Earth's rotation on its axis.

B The Earth's orbit around the Sun.

C The tilt of the Earth's axis.

D The movement of the moon around Earth.

33. What is the primary reason we experience high and low tides on Earth?

A The rotation of the Earth on its axis.

B The gravitational pull of the Moon and the Sun on Earth's oceans.

C The Earth's revolution around the Sun.

D The wind patterns over the oceans.

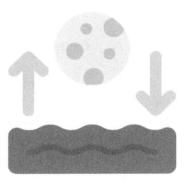

34. What is the main difference between amphibians and reptiles?

A Amphibians have feathers that are lost when they mature, and reptiles have scales all their lives.

B Amphibians lay eggs only on dry land, and reptiles give birth to live young either in water or on land.

C Amphibians have dry skin that does not require moisture, and reptiles have moist skin all of the time.

D Amphibians usually have moist skin and live in water and on land, whereas reptiles have dry, scaly skin and live primarily on land.

35. How do you think plants and animals adapt to survive in different habitats?

(A) By changing their colors.

(B) By learning new skills.

(C) By evolving physical traits.

(D) By hiding from predators.

36. A group of animals is shown:

Camel   Scorpion   Rattle Snake

Which habitat are these animals BEST suited for?

(A) A temperate grassland with fertile soil and occasional trees.

(B) A polar ice cap with frozen seas and little vegetation.

(C) A hot desert with sandy soil and sparse vegetation.

(D) A dense mangrove swamp with brackish water and tidal movements.

37. A group of students is testing how far they can throw different balls. What change will reduce the force needed to throw the balls the same distance?

(A) Use a lighter ball.

(B) Use a heavier ball.

(C) Throw the ball at a higher angle.

(D) Throw the ball at a lower angle.

74

38. When you ride a bike uphill, which force are you mostly working against?

- (A) Gravity
- (B) Air resistance
- (C) Magnetism
- (D) Friction

39. Which of these is an example of kinetic energy?

- (A) A battery-operated toy robot.
- (B) A ball thrown into the air.
- (C) A book sitting on a shelf.
- (D) A stretched rubber band.

40. The Falling Objects:

Emily and James are dropping objects from different heights to see how fast they fall.

Which object do you think will hit the ground first: a small ball or a big ball? Why?

- (A) The small ball, because it is lighter.
- (B) The big ball, because it is heavier.
- (C) Both balls will hit the ground at the same time.
- (D) It depends on how hard they are dropped.

_____

_____

_____

_____

_____

41. The circuit has five lightbulbs and four switches. If Switch 1, 2, and 4 are closed which lightbulbs will glow? Write the answer on the line provided. If none of the lightbulbs will glow, write NONE on the line: _____

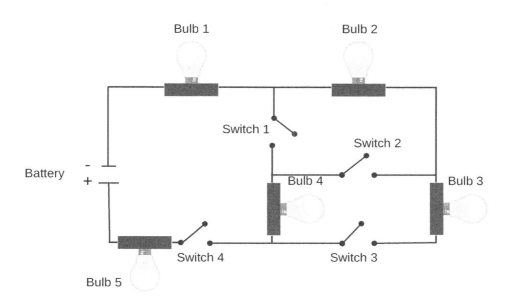

42. During a science experiment, students observe that a balloon rubbed against a wool sweater sticks to a wall. What is the most likely explanation for this phenomenon?

(A) The balloon becomes magnetic when rubbed against wool.

(B) The balloon gains a positive charge and is attracted to the negative charge on the wall.

(C) The balloon emits light that attracts it to the wall surface.

(D) The balloon absorbs moisture from the sweater, causing it to stick to the wall.

43. A student holds a flashlight in front of a mirror. What is the most likely explanation for why the student sees the light beam reflected off the mirror?

(A) The mirror absorbs the light beam.

(B) The mirror bends the light beam.

(C) The mirror transmits the light beam.

(D) The mirror reflects the light beam.

44. A student notices that the temperature decreases as they climb to the top of a mountain. What is the most likely reason for this temperature change?

(A) The mountain absorbs heat from the atmosphere.

(B) The mountain reflects heat from the Sun.

(C) The mountain refracts heat from the surroundings.

(D) The mountain experiences a decrease in air pressure, causing a decrease in temperature.

Answers Practice Test 4

1. A. Mercury

2. C. Moon

3. B. Gravitational force

4. B. To attract mates

5. C. To adapt to different environments.

6. B. Grass

7. A. Oxygen

8. A. On the leaves

9. D. Thermal energy from the air.

10. B. By storing energy and bouncing back.

11. A. Two different liquids could be water and oil.

12. A. Dandelions reproduce through seeds that disperse in the wind, while oak trees reproduce through acorns that fall to the ground.

A. Dandelions' ability to disperse seeds in the wind allows them to colonize new areas quickly and compete with other plants for resources.

13. A. Sour taste

14. B. The spoon will get warmer, and the soup will get cooler.

15. B. Use a magnet to attract the metal screws.

16. D. Sample 4 is mercury.

17. B. They have hair or fur and produce milk for their young.

18. B. Both are shaped by uplift and erosion.

19. D. Earth is the third planet from the Sun, and Mars is the fourth planet from the Sun.

20. C. The sugar cube dissolved in the coffee.

21. C. Wetlands

22. A. The Earth's axis is perpendicular to its orbit around the Sun.

23. B. Arctic regions with sea ice and tundra.

24. C. Valleys

25. C. Because they are made of different molecules.

26. C. Animal migration routes would be disrupted.

27. C. To swim and dive for food.

28. C. They create bubbles and fizz.

29. B. Earth rotates on its axis.

30. A. Comets are primarily made of ice and dust.
   C. Both comets and asteroids orbit the sun.

31. A. Mars is known as the Red Planet.
   D. Saturn is famous for its rings.

32. A. The Earth's rotation on its axis.

33. B. The gravitational pull of the Moon and the Sun on Earth's oceans.

34. D. Amphibians usually have moist skin and live in water and on land, whereas reptiles have dry, scaly skin and live primarily on land.

35. C. By evolving physical traits.

36. C. A hot desert with sandy soil and sparse vegetation.

37. A. Use a lighter ball.

38. A. Gravity

39. B. A ball thrown into the air.

40. C. Both balls will hit the ground at the same time.

Explanation: In physics, all objects fall towards the Earth at the same rate of acceleration due to gravity (approximately 9.8 meters per second squared). Therefore, regardless of their size or weight (assuming air resistance is negligible), both the small ball and the big ball will hit the ground at the same time when dropped from the same height. This scenario introduces the concept of gravity and how it affects falling objects in a straightforward manner.

41. Bulbs 1, 2, and 5.

42. B. The balloon gains a positive charge and is attracted to the negative charge on the wall.

43. D. The mirror reflects the light beam.

44. D. The mountain experiences a decrease in air pressure, causing a decrease in temperature.

PRACTICE TEST 5

GET STARTED →

1. Which planet in our solar system is known for having the most extensive and complex system of rings?

(A) Saturn

(B) Jupiter

(C) Uranus

(D) Neptune

2. What is the primary energy source for the Earth's climate and weather systems?

(A) The Moon

(B) The Sun

(C) The Earth's core

(D) The Earth's magnetic field

3. Which ocean is the largest by surface area?

(A) Atlantic Ocean

(B) Indian Ocean

(C) Arctic Ocean

(D) Pacific Ocean

4. Which of the following food chains correctly shows the flow of energy in a tundra ecosystem?

- (A) Lichens → caribou → wolves → polar bears
- (B) Polar bears → wolves → caribou → lichens
- (C) Caribou → polar bears → wolves → lichens
- (D) Lichens → wolves → polar bears → caribou

5. How does deforestation affect the environment?

- (A) Increases biodiversity.
- (B) Reduces carbon dioxide in the atmosphere.
- (C) Leads to loss of habitat, reduces biodiversity, and contributes to climate change.
- (D) Improves soil quality.

6. In a deep-sea hydrothermal vent ecosystem, what is the primary source of energy?

- (A) Crabs
- (B) Bacteria
- (C) Fish
- (D) Waves

7. Answer the question with the help of the following image. During photosynthesis, which gas is typically consumed and converted, leading to its release as a byproduct into the atmosphere?

A) Oxygen

B) Nitrogen

C) Carbon dioxide

D) Methane

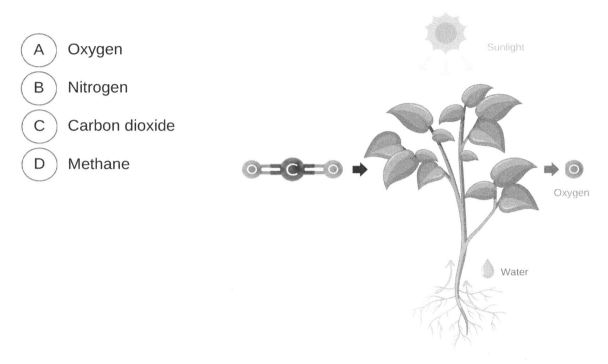

8. With the help of the image answer the question. What is the process called when tadpoles transform into adult frogs?

A) Metamorphosis

B) Evolution

C) Adaptation

D) Molt

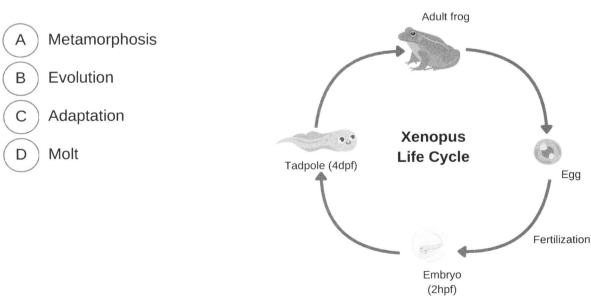

9. In a science experiment, a student observes water boiling in a kettle on a stove. Which form of energy is directly heating the water?

- (A) Mechanical energy from the stove burner.
- (B) Electrical energy from the power outlet.
- (C) Chemical energy from the water molecules.
- (D) Thermal energy from the stove burner.

10. During a demonstration, a teacher shined a laser beam through a smoke-filled room. What is the reason the laser beam becomes visible in the smoke?

- (A) The smoke particles reflect the laser light.
- (B) The laser light is absorbed by the smoke.
- (C) The laser light passes through without any interaction.
- (D) Smoke makes laser beams change color.

11. A book falls off a table and lands on the floor. What force causes the book to come to rest?

- (A) Air resistance pushing against the book.
- (B) Gravity pulling the book downward.
- (C) Friction between the book and the floor.
- (D) Elastic force from the impact of hitting the floor.

12. Students observe the picture below where particles of an unknown material are added to pure water. After mixing, the particles float in the container.

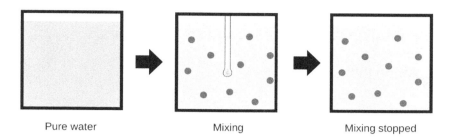

Pure water   Mixing   Mixing stopped

Which conclusion can be made from the image?

(A) Water has a higher density than the particles'.

(B) Water has a lower density than the particles'.

(C) Water has a similar density to the particles'.

(D) The particles are partially soluble in water.

13. The Balloon Race:

Sarah and Tom are blowing up balloons and racing them across the room.

Balloon A: This balloon is blown up with a small amount of air.
Balloon B: This balloon is blown up with a large amount of air.

Which balloon do you think will move faster across the room: Balloon A or Balloon B? Why?

(A) Balloon A, because it has less air.

(B) Balloon B, because it has more air.

(C) Both balloons will move at the same speed.

(D) It depends on how Sarah and Tom blow up the balloons.

_____

_____

_____

_____

_____

14. How do you think soap helps clean dirty dishes?

(A) By making them smell nice.

(B) By breaking up dirt and grease into smaller pieces.

(C) By coloring them.

(D) By making them float.

15. A student combines a mixture of sand and salt. How can the student separate the sand and salt?

(A) Dissolve the mixture in water and then filter it.

(B) Use a magnet to attract the sand particles.

(C) Heat the mixture until the sand burns away.

(D) Pour the mixture through filter paper to separate.

16. The Melting Race:

Sarah and Tom are conducting an experiment to see which substance melts faster.

Substance A: A small piece of butter.
Substance B: A small piece of chocolate.

Which substance do you think will melt faster: Substance A (butter) or Substance B (chocolate)? Why?

(A) Substance A, because it is softer.

(B) Substance B, because it is sweeter.

(C) Both substances will melt at the same rate.

(D) It depends on the temperature of the room.

_____

_____

_____

_____

_____

17. A table of the properties of four different samples of matter is shown.

Sample	Conducts Electricity	Conducts Heat	Soluble in Water	Physical State at Room Temperature
1	No	No	Yes	Solid
2	Yes	Yes	No	Solid
3	No	Yes	Yes	Liquid
4	No	Yes	Yes	Gas

Which answer is correct for sample 4?

A) Sample 4 is plastic.

B) Sample 4 is iron.

C) Sample 4 is alcohol.

D) Sample 4 is oxygen.

18. Which of the following animals is cold-blooded?

Lizard   Dog   Bird   Dolphin

A) Lizard

B) Dog

C) Bird

D) Dolphin

19. Fjord and Inlet:

Fjords and inlets are water features along coastal regions. Which statement best describes how fjords and inlets are similar?

- (A) Both are formed by sedimentary rock deposits.
- (B) Both are created by glacial erosion.
- (C) Both are results of tectonic plate movements.
- (D) Both are influenced by river deltas.

20. Which of the following correctly describes the position of Jupiter and Saturn in the solar system?

- (A) Jupiter is closer to the Sun than Saturn.
- (B) Saturn is closer to the Sun than Jupiter.
- (C) Jupiter and Saturn are the closest planets to the Sun.
- (D) Saturn is the closest planet to the Sun.

21. A student spilled colored dye onto a white fabric and then rinsed it under cold water. After rinsing, the fabric was no longer white but had taken on the color of the dye. What most likely happened to the dye?

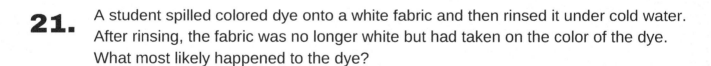

- (A) The dye evaporated from the fabric.
- (B) The dye dissolved in the water.
- (C) The dye solidified on the fabric.
- (D) The dye was absorbed into the fabric's fibers.

87

22. Imagine you are studying a reptile species. You observe the following characteristics:

- Pale coloration to reflect sunlight
- Long, slender body with scales
- Efficient kidneys to conserve water
- Burrows underground during the day
- Diet primarily consists of insects and small rodents.

Based on these characteristics, which habitat do you think this reptile is most likely adapted to live in?

- (A) Rainforest
- (B) Desert
- (C) Arctic Tundra
- (D) Grassland

23. Why do we experience shorter days in the winter?

- (A) The Earth tilts away from the Sun, resulting in less direct sunlight.
- (B) The Earth moves further away from the Sun during winter.
- (C) The Moon blocks part of the sunlight during winter.
- (D) The Earth spins faster during winter.

24. Water lilies are aquatic plants known for their floating leaves and vibrant flowers. In which aquatic environment are water lilies most likely to thrive?

- (A) Fast-flowing rivers with rocky bottoms.
- (B) Shallow ponds with muddy bottoms.
- (C) Deep lakes with sandy bottoms.
- (D) Salty marshes with brackish water.

25. A three-step process is shown:

Heat → Pressure → Recrystallization

Which of these are most likely formed by the process shown?

(A) Clouds

(B) Metamorphic rocks

(C) Water

(D) Glaciers

26. What property makes metals like aluminum and copper useful for making cooking utensils?

(A) They are brittle.

(B) They are heavy.

(C) They conduct heat well.

(D) They are transparent.

27. What would most likely be the environmental impact of expanding agricultural fields into a wetland area?

(A) Improved water quality in the wetland.

(B) Reduced habitats for wetland species.

(C) Increased biodiversity in the area.

(D) Decreased need for irrigation.

28. Students are learning about the different animals in a zoo. They focus on giraffes and record their characteristics:

Giraffe Characteristics:
- Long neck and legs for reaching high leaves
- Coat with patches of brown spots for camouflage
- Herbivorous diet primarily of leaves and buds
- Large, heart-shaped tongue for grasping leaves
- Habitat in savannas with dry grasslands and scattered trees

What is the most likely reason giraffes have a long neck?

A   To run faster.

B   To hide from predators.

C   To reach high leaves.

D   To swim in rivers.

29. Which object will float in water?

A   Wooden block.

B   Metal coin.

C   Plastic toy.

D   Rock.

30. If you drop a feather and a hammer on the Moon, where there is no air resistance, what will happen?

A   The feather will fall slower than the hammer.

B   The hammer will fall slower than the feather.

C   Both will fall at the same rate.

D   The hammer will float while the feather falls.

31. A student is studying the properties of different celestial bodies. Which statements about celestial bodies are correct? Select TWO correct answers.

(A) Black holes have strong gravitational pulls that even light cannot escape.

(B) Planets have their own light sources.

(C) Moons always have an atmosphere.

(D) Nebulas are clouds of gas and dust in space.

(E) Comets remain stationary in space.

32. Which of the following describes the primary reason for the difference in temperature between day and night on Earth?

(A) The Earth's rotation on its axis.

(B) The Earth's revolution around the Sun.

(C) The Sun moving closer to and farther from Earth.

(D) The moon blocking the Sun's light at night.

33. Which statements correctly describe the characteristics of Earth and the moon? Select TWO correct answers.

(A) Earth has a breathable atmosphere, while the moon does not.

(B) The moon produces its own light, while Earth does not.

(C) Earth has liquid water, while the moon does not.

(D) The moon is larger than Earth.

(E) Earth and the moon have the same gravity.

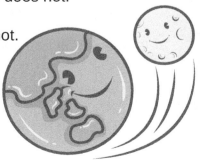

34. Why do we have a leap year every four years?

A) Because the Earth's orbit around the Sun takes 365.25 days.

B) Because the moon's orbit around Earth affects our calendar.

C) Because the Sun's energy output changes every four years.

D) Because of changes in Earth's axial tilt.

35. What is the largest land animal on Earth?

A) Blue Whale

B) African Elephant

C) Giraffe

D) Hippopotamus

36. The Plant Growth Experiment:

Sarah and Jack are experimenting with different amounts of sunlight on plant growth.

Sarah places one plant in a sunny window and another plant in a dark cupboard. What do you think will happen to each plant over time?

A) The plant in the sunny window will grow taller because it receives more sunlight for photosynthesis.

B) The plant in the dark cupboard will grow taller because it conserves energy without sunlight.

C) Both plants will grow at the same rate because they are the same type of plant.

D) It depends on the type of plants Sarah is growing.

_____

_____

_____

_____

37. A group of animals is shown.

Tiger   Monkey   Snake

Which habitat are these animals BEST suited for?

- (A) A dense rainforest with tall trees and thick underbrush.
- (B) A polar ice cap with frozen seas and little vegetation.
- (C) A hot desert with sand dunes and cacti.
- (D) A shallow estuary with brackish water and tidal movements.

38. A student is pushing a shopping cart across a parking lot. What change will reduce the amount of force needed to move the shopping cart?

- (A) Increase the weight of the items in the cart.
- (B) Decrease the size of the wheels on the cart.
- (C) Push the cart on a rougher surface.
- (D) Push the cart with a longer handle.

39. What type of energy is stored in a stretched rubber band?

- (A) Kinetic energy
- (B) Thermal energy
- (C) Potential energy
- (D) Mechanical energy

40. Which force keeps planets in orbit around the Sun?

(A) Friction

(B) Gravity

(C) Tension

(D) Air resistance

41. Students want to investigate how the angle of a ramp affects the speed of a toy car rolling down on it. Which procedure should they follow for their experiment?

(A) Measure the speed of the toy car rolling down ramps of different angles. Conduct three trials for each angle.

(B) Measure the speed of the toy car rolling down the same ramp at different times of the day. Conduct three trials for each time.

(C) Measure the speed of the toy car rolling down ramps of different angles using different toy cars. Conduct three trials for each car.

(D) Measure the speed of the toy car rolling down the same ramp at the same angle using different students. Conduct three trials for each student.

42. The circuit has five lightbulbs and four switches. If Switch 1 and 2 are closed which lightbulbs will glow? Write the answer on the line provided. If none of the lightbulbs will glow, write NONE on the line: _____

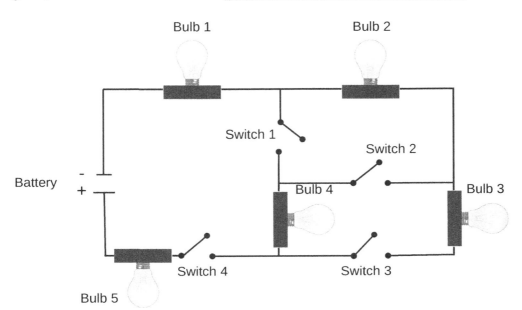

43. This question has two parts. First, answer Part A. Then, based on your answer to Part A, answer Part B.

Part A
A student studies two planets: Mars and Jupiter. Which statement BEST describes a key difference between Mars and Jupiter?

(A) Jupiter is a rocky planet with a thin atmosphere, while Mars is a gas giant with thick clouds of hydrogen and helium.

(B) Mars has rings made of ice and rock particles, while Jupiter has no visible rings around its equator.

(C) Mars orbits closer to the Sun and has a reddish appearance due to iron oxide on its surface, while Jupiter orbits farther away and appears as a bright, striped gas giant.

(D) Mars has a solid surface covered with water oceans, while Jupiter has a turbulent surface with active volcanoes.

Part B
Based on your answer to Part A, which statement BEST explains how this difference in appearance or orbit helps each planet?

(A) Mars' closer orbit to the Sun results in higher temperatures, which help maintain its iron-rich surface coloration.

(B) Mars's position farther from the Sun allows for a colder environment, which promotes the formation of its extensive cloud layers.

(C) Mars' reddish appearance makes it less visible to telescopes compared to Jupiter's bright clouds, which aids in studying its surface features.

(D) Jupiter's striped appearance is caused by the planet's rapid rotation and strong magnetic field, which create distinct atmospheric bands.

44. What happens to the particles in a substance when it is heated?

(A) They move slower and get closer together.

(B) They move faster and spread apart.

(C) They stop moving completely.

(D) They change shape.

Answers Practice Test 5

1. A. Saturn
2. B. The Sun
3. D. Pacific Ocean
4. A. Lichens → caribou → wolves → polar bears
5. C. Leads to loss of habitat, reduces biodiversity, and contributes to climate change.
6. B. Bacteria
7. C. Carbon dioxide
8. A. Metamorphosis
9. D. Thermal energy from the stove burner.
10. A. The smoke particles reflect the laser light.
11. B. Gravity pulling the book downward.
12. C. Water has a similar density to the particles'.
13. B. Balloon B, because it has more air.
Explanation: In physics, the motion of an object propelled by air (like a balloon) depends on the amount of air (mass) and the force exerted (thrust). Balloon B, being larger and filled with more air, experiences a greater force of propulsion when released, resulting in faster movement across the room compared to Balloon A, which has less air and therefore less force. This scenario introduces the concept of thrust and mass affecting the motion of objects propelled by air in a fun and interactive context.
14. B. By breaking up dirt and grease into smaller pieces.
15. A. Dissolve the mixture in water and then filter it.
16. A. Substance A, because it is softer.
Explanation: In chemistry, the melting point of a substance refers to the temperature at which it changes from a solid to a liquid state. Generally, substances with lower melting points will melt faster at room temperature compared to substances with higher melting points. Butter (Substance A) typically has a lower melting point than chocolate (Substance B) due to its composition of fats and water content.
Therefore, Butter (Substance A) is expected to melt faster when exposed to the same environmental conditions.
17. D. Sample 5 is oxygen.
18. A. Lizard
19. B. Both are created by glacial erosion.
20. A. Jupiter is closer to the sun than Saturn.
21. D. The dye was absorbed into the fabric's fibers.
22. B. Desert
23. A. The Earth tilts away from the Sun, resulting in less direct sunlight.
24. B. Shallow ponds with muddy bottoms.
25. B. Metamorphic rocks

26. C. They conduct heat well.
27. B. Reduced habitats for wetland species.
28. C. To reach high leaves.
29. C. Plastic toy
30. B. Both will fall at the same rate.
31. A. Black holes have strong gravitational pulls that even light cannot escape.
   D. Nebulas are clouds of gas and dust in space.
32. A. The Earth's rotation on its axis.
33. A. Earth has a breathable atmosphere, while the moon does not.
   C. Earth has liquid water, while the moon does not.
34. A. Because the Earth's orbit around the sun takes 365.25 days.
35. B. African Elephant
36. A. The plant in the sunny window will grow taller because it receives more sunlight for photosynthesis.
Explanation: In biology, sunlight is crucial for photosynthesis, the process by which plants convert light energy into chemical energy (glucose) to fuel their growth and development. Plants placed in sunny locations receive more energy from sunlight, allowing them to produce more glucose and grow taller compared to plants in low-light conditions.
37. A. A dense rainforest with tall trees and thick underbrush.
38. D. Push the cart with a longer handle.
39. C. Potential energy
40. B. Gravity
41. A. Measure the speed of the toy car rolling down ramps of different angles. Conduct three trials for each angle.
42. NONE
43. C. Mars orbits closer to the Sun and has a reddish appearance due to iron oxide on its surface, while Jupiter orbits farther away and appears as a bright, striped gas giant.
   A. Mars' closer orbit to the Sun results in higher temperatures, which help maintain its iron-rich surface coloration.
44. B. They move faster and spread apart.

96

Made in United States
Orlando, FL
10 April 2025